VGM's Careers Checklists

VGM's Careers Checklists

89 PROVEN CHECKLISTS TO HELP YOU PLAN YOUR CAREER AND GET GREAT JOBS

Arlene S. Hirsch

VGM Career Horizons
a division of *NTC Publishing Group*
Lincolnwood, Illinois USA

Library of Congress Cataloging-in-Publication Data

Hirsch, Arlene S., 1951–
  VGM's careers checklists / by Arlene S. Hirsch.

    p. cm.
  ISBN 0-8442-8557-9 : $9.95
  1. Vocational guidance—Handbooks, manuals, etc. 2. Job hunting—
—Handbooks, manuals, etc. 3. Career development—Handbooks,
manuals, etc. I. Title.
HF5381H517   1990
650.14—dc20

90-36810
CIP

Published by VGM Career Horizons, a division of NTC Publishing Group.
©1991 by NTC Publishing Group, 4255 West Touhy Avenue,
Lincolnwood (Chicago), Illinois 60646-1975 U.S.A.
Manufactured in the United States of America.

0 1 2 3 4 5 6 7 8 9 VP 9 8 7 6 5 4 3 2 1

Contents

Chapter 3: Job-Search Strategies and Techniques   103

Chapter 4: Successful Interviews   149

Chapter 5: Changing Careers   **173**

Chapter 6: Checking Your Progress   **189**

About the Author ———

Arlene S. Hirsch is a career counselor and psychotherapist in private practice. She works with individuals who are experiencing career or personal problems. Her services include individual consultations, vocational testing, workshops, support groups, and résumé preparation.

A graduate of Northwestern University, she received her master's degree in counseling psychology in 1983. A career changer herself, she has also worked in management and teaching before entering the field of psychology and career development.

Since starting her private practice, Ms. Hirsch has lectured extensively to professional organizations and consulted to corporations, government agencies, social service agencies, and educational institutions. She has appeared on both radio and television to discuss career-related topics.

In addition to her private practice, Ms. Hirsch teaches adult career development at DePaul University. She is the author of "ShopTalk," a weekly career advice column published by the Chicagoland Job Source. Her articles have also appeared in Business Week and Wall Street Journal publications.

Acknowledgments

When I first saw the movie *Three Men and a Baby*, I was touched, amused, and charmed by the heartwarming efforts of three grown men to care for a newborn baby. (Fortunately, the baby survived their care.) I, too, am indebted to three men for their generous efforts to nurture my development.

To my brother, Eddie Hirsch—first hero, first protector. To Sonny Cytrynbaum—inspiring teacher, early believer. To Tony Lee—an editor who saw promise in my work.

A fourth man deserves special recognition. This book is dedicated to Dr. Jesse Viner for his unique contribution to my personal and professional development. His boundless patience, tenacity, compassion, and wisdom are a constant source of comfort and guidance.

Charting Your Career Path

"Nothing great was ever achieved
without enthusiasm."

—Aristotle

1. The 10 Commandments of Career Success

1. Choose work you love.

2. Develop competence.

3. Learn self-confidence.

4. Be assertive.

5. Take risks.

6. Strive for visibility.

7. Take credit for success.

8. Accept responsibility (whatever happens).

9. Be a team player.

10. Develop a sense of humor—you'll need it.

2. 6-Step Career Development Process

The following six steps will help guide a lifetime of career development. They are an ongoing checklist of actions to take, so you should refer back to them regularly.

☐ 1. Develop an active approach to career development. First and foremost, recognize that you have complete responsibility for your career development.

☐ 2. Conduct a self-assessment that includes a thorough evaluation of interests, skills, values, needs, and personality. This will lay the foundation for you to identify conditions and opportunities that will be satisfying for you.

☐ 3. Arm yourself with career information. In an information-intensive workplace, knowledge is power. Keep abreast of workplace trends, career opportunities, and potential options through reading and talking. The more you know, the more secure you will be.

☐ 4. Develop a long-term perspective. Recognizing that people change throughout the life cycle means that you must constantly evaluate your skills, interests, values, needs, and options. Gone are the days of the "one-career, one-company" mentality. People today voluntarily and involuntarily move around a lot more often.

☐ 5. Learn good job-search skills so that you will be less vulnerable and have more options available to you. People who know how to look for work don't need to get locked into "golden handcuffs" or fear job loss, because they know they can find another job. There is no greater peace of mind than that.

☐ 6. Build a network and keep it alive. Some of the best inside information is communicated by word of mouth. Make it an ongoing practice to know what's happening so that you can prepare yourself for changes and, if you do get caught off guard, you can activate your network instantaneously.

3. 15 Work-Related Values

Recognizing your values is an important part of your self-assessment. Review the following list of work-related values. Rank them from 1 through 15 (1 = most important, 15 = least important). If there are other values that you consider important but are not included in this list, write them in at the bottom and include them in your ranking, adding numbers to encompass the total number of values listed. Then look at your top five choices. What can you conclude about your values based on these choices? Briefly write your conclusion in the *Values Summary* section at the end of this worksheet.

_____ wealth

_____ security

_____ independence

_____ making a contribution to society

_____ expertness

_____ creativity

_____ helping others

_____ variety

_____ affiliation

_____ growth

_____ self-fulfillment

_____ recognition

_____ power

_____ challenge

_____ other: _____

_____ other: _____

_____ other: _____

Values Summary

_____

_____

_____

_____

_____

_____

_____

_____

_____

HINT: Look inside yourself for answers before you look to the job market. If you don't know what you are looking for, you will have trouble finding it.

4. Interest Inventory

Your interests (likes and dislikes) are an important part of every career choice you make. People who do not develop or utilize their interests in their career will often find their work boring.

List 10 activities you particularly enjoy.

1. _____
2. _____
3. _____
4. _____
5. _____
6. _____
7. _____
8. _____
9. _____
10. _____

List 10 school subjects you most like to study.

1. _____
2. _____
3. _____
4. _____
5. _____
6. _____
7. _____

8. _____

9. _____

10. _____

List 10 occupations that interest you.

1. _____

2. _____

3. _____

4. _____

5. _____

6. _____

7. _____

8. _____

9. _____

10. _____

Use the checklist below to stimulate your thinking. Place a check mark next
to things you like to do, play, study, or watch.

☐ acting	☐ athletics	☐ chemistry
☐ activism	☐ baking	☐ children
☐ advertising	☐ biology	☐ clothing
☐ advising	☐ bookkeeping	☐ communicating
☐ animals	☐ building	☐ computers
☐ agriculture	☐ business	☐ cooking
☐ architecture	☐ buying	☐ counseling
☐ art		☐ crafts
	☐ cars	
☐ astronomy		
	☐ carpentry	☐ dance

- [ ] debate
- [ ] drawing
- [ ] driving

- [ ] educating/education
- [ ] entertaining

- [ ] farming
- [ ] fashion
- [ ] fixing/repairing
- [ ] flowers
- [ ] flying
- [ ] foreign languages

- [ ] gambling
- [ ] gardening

- [ ] healing
- [ ] homemaking

- [ ] interior design
- [ ] interviewing
- [ ] investigating
- [ ] investing

- [ ] jewelry
- [ ] journalism

- [ ] law
- [ ] libraries

- [ ] machinery/tools
- [ ] magazines
- [ ] mathematics
- [ ] medical science
- [ ] medical service
- [ ] military activities
- [ ] moneymaking
- [ ] movies
- [ ] museums
- [ ] music

- [ ] nature
- [ ] newspapers

- [ ] outdoor activities

- [ ] painting
- [ ] philosophy
- [ ] photography
- [ ] plays
- [ ] politics
- [ ] problem-solving
- [ ] psychology

- [ ] public speaking

- [ ] radio
- [ ] reading
- [ ] real estate
- [ ] religion
- [ ] research

- [ ] science
- [ ] sales/selling
- [ ] sewing
- [ ] shopping
- [ ] social service
- [ ] social studies
- [ ] sports
- [ ] statistics
- [ ] stock market
- [ ] studying

- [ ] teaching
- [ ] television
- [ ] travel
- [ ] typing

- [ ] writing

Now, go back to the lists you made at the beginning of this interest exercise. Is there anything else you would like to include?

_____

_____

_____

_____

_____

_____

_____

_____

_____

_____

5. Personality Profile

Place a check mark next to each personality characteristic that reminds you of yourself. You may want to ask a relative, friend, or colleague to fill in an identical form describing your personality, then compare notes. Look over your completed list. What conclusions can you draw about the characteristics you checked off? Briefly state your conclusions in the *Personality Summary* section at the end of this exercise. Also note how your list differs from your friend's list for you.

Personality Characteristics

☐ active

☐ adaptable

☐ adventurous

☐ adversarial

☐ affectionate

☐ aggressive

☐ aloof

☐ ambitious

☐ amiable

☐ analytical

☐ angry

☐ antagonistic

☐ anxious

☐ apologetic

☐ asleep

☐ assertive

☐ authoritative

☐ benign

☐ blunt

☐ boastful

☐ boisterous

☐ bold

☐ bookish

☐ boring

☐ bossy

☐ bottom-liner

☐ brave

☐ bright

☐ broadminded

☐ businesslike

☐ cagey

- [ ] calculating
- [ ] calm
- [ ] candid
- [ ] capricious
- [ ] carefree
- [ ] careful
- [ ] careless
- [ ] cavalier
- [ ] centered
- [ ] charismatic
- [ ] charming
- [ ] chauvinistic
- [ ] cheap
- [ ] cheerful
- [ ] childlike
- [ ] chivalrous
- [ ] classy
- [ ] companionable
- [ ] compassionate
- [ ] complacent
- [ ] complex
- [ ] con artist
- [ ] concerned
- [ ] conformist
- [ ] conscientious
- [ ] conservative

- [ ] considerate
- [ ] content
- [ ] contrary
- [ ] controversial
- [ ] cooperative
- [ ] courageous
- [ ] creative
- [ ] critical
- [ ] cultured
- [ ] cunning
- [ ] curious
- [ ] cynical

- [ ] daring
- [ ] daydreamer
- [ ] deceitful
- [ ] dedicated
- [ ] defensive
- [ ] dependable
- [ ] dependent
- [ ] depressed
- [ ] determined
- [ ] dictatorial
- [ ] different
- [ ] dignified
- [ ] direct

- [ ] disciplined
- [ ] discreet
- [ ] disillusioned
- [ ] docile

- [ ] eager
- [ ] earnest
- [ ] earthy
- [ ] easygoing
- [ ] ebullient
- [ ] eccentric
- [ ] educated
- [ ] effective
- [ ] efficient
- [ ] effusive
- [ ] egotistical
- [ ] elitist
- [ ] eloquent
- [ ] emotional
- [ ] empathic
- [ ] emphatic
- [ ] energetic
- [ ] engaging
- [ ] enthusiastic
- [ ] evasive
- [ ] exasperating

- [ ] expansive
- [ ] explosive
- [ ] extremist

- [ ] factual
- [ ] fair
- [ ] fearful
- [ ] fearless
- [ ] flaky
- [ ] flexible
- [ ] focused
- [ ] foolhardy
- [ ] foresightful
- [ ] Frankenstein
- [ ] freethinker
- [ ] friendly
- [ ] frugal

- [ ] generous
- [ ] genteel
- [ ] gentle
- [ ] genuine
- [ ] gloomy
- [ ] go-getter
- [ ] goodnatured
- [ ] goody-goody

- [ ] gossipy
- [ ] gracious
- [ ] gregarious
- [ ] gross
- [ ] grumpy
- [ ] guilty

- [ ] happy-go-lucky
- [ ] happy
- [ ] hardheaded
- [ ] hardhearted
- [ ] hasty
- [ ] helpful
- [ ] helpless
- [ ] homebody
- [ ] honest
- [ ] hostile
- [ ] human
- [ ] humane
- [ ] humble
- [ ] humorless
- [ ] humorous

- [ ] idealistic
- [ ] impatient
- [ ] impervious

- [ ] impressionable
- [ ] inconsiderate
- [ ] independent
- [ ] intelligent
- [ ] inhibited
- [ ] initiator
- [ ] innocent
- [ ] insensitive
- [ ] insightful
- [ ] insincere
- [ ] intellectual
- [ ] intense
- [ ] introspective
- [ ] introverted
- [ ] intuitive
- [ ] irrational
- [ ] irritable

- [ ] jittery
- [ ] jolly
- [ ] judgmental
- [ ] judicious

- [ ] kind
- [ ] knowledgeable

- [ ] lazy

- [ ] leader
- [ ] lethargic
- [ ] lighthearted
- [ ] lively
- [ ] looney-tunes
- [ ] loner

- [ ] malicious
- [ ] manic
- [ ] manipulative
- [ ] melancholy
- [ ] mercenary
- [ ] misfit
- [ ] modest
- [ ] motivated
- [ ] myopic

- [ ] naive
- [ ] narcissistic
- [ ] narrowminded
- [ ] needy
- [ ] negative
- [ ] nervous
- [ ] neurotic
- [ ] nice
- [ ] nocturnal

- [ ] nonconformist
- [ ] nosy
- [ ] nutty

- [ ] objective
- [ ] obsequious
- [ ] obstinate
- [ ] open-minded
- [ ] optimistic
- [ ] organized
- [ ] outgoing

- [ ] paranoid
- [ ] passive
- [ ] patient
- [ ] pennywise
- [ ] perceptive
- [ ] personable
- [ ] persuasive
- [ ] petulant
- [ ] philosophical
- [ ] physical
- [ ] pioneering
- [ ] placid
- [ ] playful
- [ ] pleasant

- ☐ pliant
- ☐ poised
- ☐ polite
- ☐ polished
- ☐ possessive
- ☐ practical
- ☐ precise
- ☐ principled
- ☐ professional
- ☐ prompt
- ☐ protective
- ☐ provocative
- ☐ prudent
- ☐ public-spirited

- ☐ quick-tempered
- ☐ quick-witted
- ☐ quiet
- ☐ quitter

- ☐ rational
- ☐ realistic
- ☐ rebellious
- ☐ reserved
- ☐ resilient
- ☐ respectful

- ☐ restrained
- ☐ risk-taker
- ☐ romantic

- ☐ saboteur
- ☐ sad
- ☐ sceptical
- ☐ seductive
- ☐ self-confident
- ☐ self-conscious
- ☐ self-controlled
- ☐ self-destructive
- ☐ self-determined
- ☐ self-educated
- ☐ self-effacing
- ☐ self-important
- ☐ self-pitying
- ☐ self-righteous
- ☐ self-satisfied
- ☐ self-serving
- ☐ sensitive
- ☐ serious
- ☐ settled
- ☐ sharp
- ☐ showoff

- [ ] shrewd
- [ ] shy
- [ ] silly
- [ ] smug
- [ ] snobbish
- [ ] social
- [ ] sophisticated
- [ ] softhearted
- [ ] soft-spoken
- [ ] soulful
- [ ] spiritual
- [ ] spontaneous
- [ ] spunky
- [ ] stodgy
- [ ] straightforward
- [ ] streetsmart
- [ ] strong
- [ ] stubborn
- [ ] successful
- [ ] suspicious
- [ ] sweet
- [ ] sympathetic

- [ ] tactful
- [ ] team player
- [ ] temperamental

- [ ] tenacious
- [ ] tense
- [ ] tentative
- [ ] thorough
- [ ] thrifty
- [ ] tight-lipped
- [ ] tolerant
- [ ] tranquil
- [ ] troublemaker
- [ ] troubleshooter
- [ ] trustworthy
- [ ] truthful
- [ ] two-faced
- [ ] tyrannical

- [ ] unrealistic
- [ ] unreliable
- [ ] unsympathetic
- [ ] utilitarian

- [ ] vain
- [ ] vigilant
- [ ] vocal
- [ ] volatile
- [ ] vulnerable

- [ ] weak

- [ ] well-rounded
- [ ] whistle-blower
- [ ] willful
- [ ] worldly

- [ ] youthful
- [ ] zany
- [ ] zestful

Personality Summary

_____

_____

_____

_____

_____

_____

_____

_____

_____

_____

_____

6. Skills and Abilities Checklist

It is very important to be able to identify your best skills and abilities. While you are using the checklist below to determine your strongest skills, you may also want to consider which skills you most enjoy using. You may find that you have developed some skills you do not particularly like. This will be important information for you to process during your next career transition. Look over your completed list, then summarize your strongest skills and those you enjoy most in the sections at the end of this worksheet. Are they the same?

Skill	How Long?	Level of Competence	Enjoy?
☐ accounting	_____	_____	_____
☐ administering	_____	_____	_____
☐ advising	_____	_____	_____
☐ analyzing	_____	_____	_____
☐ appraising	_____	_____	_____
☐ arbitrating	_____	_____	_____
☐ assessing	_____	_____	_____
☐ auditing	_____	_____	_____
☐ balancing	_____	_____	_____
☐ beautifying	_____	_____	_____
☐ bookkeeping	_____	_____	_____
☐ budgeting	_____	_____	_____
☐ buffering	_____	_____	_____
☐ buying	_____	_____	_____

Skill	How Long?	Level of Competence	Enjoy?
☐ calculating	_____	_____	_____
☐ canvassing	_____	_____	_____
☐ cataloguing	_____	_____	_____
☐ charting	_____	_____	_____
☐ checking	_____	_____	_____
☐ clarifying	_____	_____	_____
☐ classifying	_____	_____	_____
☐ clerical	_____	_____	_____
☐ client relations	_____	_____	_____
☐ coaching	_____	_____	_____
☐ collaborating	_____	_____	_____
☐ communicating	_____	_____	_____
☐ community relations	_____	_____	_____
☐ compiling data	_____	_____	_____
☐ computer programming	_____	_____	_____
☐ conceptualizing	_____	_____	_____
☐ conflict management	_____	_____	_____
☐ conflict resolution	_____	_____	_____
☐ consulting	_____	_____	_____
☐ coordinating	_____	_____	_____
☐ counseling	_____	_____	_____
☐ creating	_____	_____	_____
☐ crisis intervention	_____	_____	_____
☐ customer relations	_____	_____	_____

Skill	How Long?	Level of Competence	Enjoy?
☐ debating	_____	_____	_____
☐ decision making	_____	_____	_____
☐ defending	_____	_____	_____
☐ delegating	_____	_____	_____
☐ demonstrating	_____	_____	_____
☐ designing	_____	_____	_____
☐ developing people	_____	_____	_____
☐ developing procedures	_____	_____	_____
☐ developing programs	_____	_____	_____
☐ developing systems	_____	_____	_____
☐ diagnosing	_____	_____	_____
☐ diplomacy/tact	_____	_____	_____
☐ directing	_____	_____	_____
☐ doing	_____	_____	_____
☐ drafting	_____	_____	_____
☐ drawing	_____	_____	_____
☐ editing	_____	_____	_____
☐ effecting change	_____	_____	_____
☐ elaborating	_____	_____	_____
☐ employing	_____	_____	_____
☐ enforcing	_____	_____	_____
☐ enlarging	_____	_____	_____
☐ evaluating	_____	_____	_____
☐ expanding	_____	_____	_____

Skill	How Long?	Level of Competence	Enjoy?
☐ experimenting	_____	_____	_____
☐ facilitating	_____	_____	_____
☐ fighting	_____	_____	_____
☐ finalizing	_____	_____	_____
☐ financial planning	_____	_____	_____
☐ financing	_____	_____	_____
☐ following directions	_____	_____	_____
☐ following through	_____	_____	_____
☐ forecasting	_____	_____	_____
☐ formulating policy	_____	_____	_____
☐ formulating strategy	_____	_____	_____
☐ fundraising	_____	_____	_____
☐ getting along with others	_____	_____	_____
☐ globetrotting	_____	_____	_____
☐ goal setting	_____	_____	_____
☐ good manners	_____	_____	_____
☐ governing	_____	_____	_____
☐ grooming	_____	_____	_____
☐ guiding	_____	_____	_____
☐ handling responsibility	_____	_____	_____
☐ helping others	_____	_____	_____
☐ human relations	_____	_____	_____
☐ hypothesizing	_____	_____	_____

Skill	How Long?	Level of Competence	Enjoy?
☐ identifying	_____	_____	_____
☐ illustrating	_____	_____	_____
☐ implementing	_____	_____	_____
☐ influencing	_____	_____	_____
☐ initiating	_____	_____	_____
☐ innovating	_____	_____	_____
☐ instructing	_____	_____	_____
☐ integrating	_____	_____	_____
☐ interpreting	_____	_____	_____
☐ interviewing	_____	_____	_____
☐ interrogating	_____	_____	_____
☐ intervening	_____	_____	_____
☐ inventing	_____	_____	_____
☐ investing	_____	_____	_____
☐ itemizing	_____	_____	_____
☐ joining activities	_____	_____	_____
☐ joining forces	_____	_____	_____
☐ judging performance	_____	_____	_____
☐ judging quality	_____	_____	_____
☐ justifying	_____	_____	_____
☐ leading	_____	_____	_____
☐ learning	_____	_____	_____
☐ letter writing	_____	_____	_____

Skill	How Long?	Level of Competence	Enjoy?
☐ listening	_____	_____	_____
☐ maintaining	_____	_____	_____
☐ managing money	_____	_____	_____
☐ managing people	_____	_____	_____
☐ managing projects	_____	_____	_____
☐ marketing	_____	_____	_____
☐ measuring	_____	_____	_____
☐ mediating	_____	_____	_____
☐ mentoring	_____	_____	_____
☐ modifying	_____	_____	_____
☐ molding	_____	_____	_____
☐ motivating	_____	_____	_____
☐ navigating	_____	_____	_____
☐ negotiating	_____	_____	_____
☐ nurturing	_____	_____	_____
☐ observing	_____	_____	_____
☐ orchestrating	_____	_____	_____
☐ organizing	_____	_____	_____
☐ orienting	_____	_____	_____
☐ outsmarting	_____	_____	_____
☐ performing	_____	_____	_____
☐ persisting	_____	_____	_____

Skill	How Long?	Level of Competence	Enjoy?
☐ pinch-hitting	_____	_____	_____
☐ pitching in	_____	_____	_____
☐ placating	_____	_____	_____
☐ planning	_____	_____	_____
☐ policing	_____	_____	_____
☐ policy analysis	_____	_____	_____
☐ policy development	_____	_____	_____
☐ preparing	_____	_____	_____
☐ presenting	_____	_____	_____
☐ problem analysis	_____	_____	_____
☐ problem solving	_____	_____	_____
☐ program design	_____	_____	_____
☐ program development	_____	_____	_____
☐ project development	_____	_____	_____
☐ project management	_____	_____	_____
☐ promoting	_____	_____	_____
☐ public speaking	_____	_____	_____
☐ qualifying	_____	_____	_____
☐ questioning	_____	_____	_____
☐ reading	_____	_____	_____
☐ recruiting	_____	_____	_____
☐ reducing costs	_____	_____	_____
☐ reevaluating	_____	_____	_____

Skill	How Long?	Level of Competence	Enjoy?
☐ reexamining	_____	_____	_____
☐ regulating	_____	_____	_____
☐ reporting	_____	_____	_____
☐ representing	_____	_____	_____
☐ researching	_____	_____	_____
☐ reviewing	_____	_____	_____
☐ rewriting	_____	_____	_____
☐ risk taking	_____	_____	_____
☐ sacrificing	_____	_____	_____
☐ satisfying	_____	_____	_____
☐ scheduling	_____	_____	_____
☐ scrutinizing	_____	_____	_____
☐ selling	_____	_____	_____
☐ servicing	_____	_____	_____
☐ setting priorities	_____	_____	_____
☐ setting standards	_____	_____	_____
☐ solving	_____	_____	_____
☐ straightening out	_____	_____	_____
☐ strategizing	_____	_____	_____
☐ strengthening	_____	_____	_____
☐ styling	_____	_____	_____
☐ surveying	_____	_____	_____
☐ system design	_____	_____	_____
☐ supervising	_____	_____	_____

Skill	How Long?	Level of Competence	Enjoy?
☐ teaching	_____	_____	_____
☐ testing	_____	_____	_____
☐ training	_____	_____	_____
☐ traveling	_____	_____	_____
☐ troubleshooting	_____	_____	_____
☐ trying	_____	_____	_____
☐ turning things around	_____	_____	_____
☐ typing	_____	_____	_____
☐ understanding	_____	_____	_____
☐ unifying	_____	_____	_____
☐ utilizing	_____	_____	_____
☐ verbalizing	_____	_____	_____
☐ verifying	_____	_____	_____
☐ visualizing	_____	_____	_____
☐ watching	_____	_____	_____
☐ winning	_____	_____	_____
☐ word processing	_____	_____	_____
☐ writing	_____	_____	_____

My Strongest Skills

_____

_____

_____

_____

_____

_____

_____

_____

My Most Enjoyable Skills

_____

_____

_____

_____

_____

_____

_____

_____

7. Working Conditions

Although you may not get everything you want, it is always important to determine your work priorities. Then when you do go job hunting, you will try to select and negotiate positions that include as many of your work priorities as possible.

Put a "1" next to those working conditions you strongly prefer; a "2" next to those conditions you find moderately important; and a "3" next to things irrelevant or unimportant to your work happiness.

After you've completed the list, go back and look at all the items you marked with a "1". What can you conclude about your preferences? Briefly write your conclusion in the *My Preferred Working Conditions* section at the end of the list.

- ☐ a short commute
- ☐ dress code
- ☐ private office
- ☐ strict rules
- ☐ recreational facilities
- ☐ good benefits
- ☐ job security
- ☐ reasonable hours
- ☐ privacy
- ☐ feedback
- ☐ windows
- ☐ employee parking
- ☐ nice offices, surroundings
- ☐ variety
- ☐ structured work tasks
- ☐ new challenges
- ☐ room for advancement
- ☐ liberal vacation policies
- ☐ sick leave
- ☐ holiday pay
- ☐ profit sharing
- ☐ insurance benefits
- ☐ pension plan
- ☐ on-the-job training
- ☐ good relationships with coworkers
- ☐ good relationship with bosses
- ☐ high pressure
- ☐ fast pace
- ☐ smoking policy

- ☐ kitchen
- ☐ coffee
- ☐ cafeteria
- ☐ long lunch hour
- ☐ clear job description
- ☐ structured work hours
- ☐ competitive environment
- ☐ good location
- ☐ relaxed atmosphere

My Preferred Working Conditions

_____

_____

_____

_____

_____

_____

_____

_____

_____

8. Putting It All Together

Personal and professional accomplishments usually integrate skills, interests, and personality traits. Because they blend together, it may be difficult to identify and extract the different variables that contribute to each accomplishment. However, it is important to be able to analyze your accomplishments. This will enable you to determine where there may be discord between your preferred skills, interests, values, and/or personality traits. It should also enable you to think about your accomplishments in a more analytical way; then you can reorganize that information to create a more satisfying career plan.

In the next self-assessment exercise, write down 5 to 10 *specific* accomplishments. Then, analyze each accomplishment in terms of skills, interests, and personality traits that you used.

SAMPLE

Accomplishment
After I graduated from college, I wanted to go to a good graduate school in psychology. Unfortunately, I had taken very few psychology courses and had never worked in the field, so I did not have professional references. Also, my overall grade point average was only a C + . I had taken the graduate admissions exams and performed okay, but nothing spectacular.

On my application to graduate schools, I wrote a very heartfelt essay explaining why I had chosen that particular program and why it was important to go to a high-quality school. I was granted a personal interview with the program director, where I convinced him to give me a try. I was then admitted to the program as a "special student," which meant that I would have the opportunity to prove I could really do the work. I studied very hard and aced both courses by writing good research papers and getting involved in class discussions. When it was time to reapply to the program, the director wrote a personal recommendation for me and later became my academic advisor.

Analysis

Skills used: adaptability, building (credibility), communicating, compiling data, cultivating (contacts), defending (my candidacy), effecting (change of attitude), familiarizing (teachers with my qualifications), following directions, following through, formulating (a plan), getting along with others, growing, handling, human relations, illustrating, influencing, initiating, interpersonal, interrelating, interviewing, justifying, learning, letter-writing, listening, modifying, negotiating, observing, organizing, performing, persisting, persuading, planning, preparing, problem solving, promoting (self), proving (I could handle the coursework), qualifying, questioning, reading, representing, researching, rewriting, risk taking, sacrificing (income), salvaging (a poor undergraduate record), selling (myself), strengthening (my credentials), tolerating anxiety, troubleshooting, typing, understanding, verbalizing, watching, winning, writing.

Interests: counseling, education, psychology, research, writing.

Personality traits: active, adaptable, adventurous, ambitious, analytical, assertive, bright, conscientious, cooperative, creative, curious, dedicated, dependable, determined, eager, empathic, energetic, enthusiastic, flexible, friendly, genuine, go-getter, honest, human, idealistic, independent, intelligent, initiator, insightful, intellectual, motivated, nice, nonconformist, optimistic, patient, perceptive, personable, persuasive, pleasant, poised, principled, respectful, risk-taker, self-determined, sensitive, serious, strong, trustworthy, vocal.

Values: intellectual challenge, competence, growth, self-expression, helping others, making a contribution to society, organizational identification.

Accomplishment #1: _____

_____

_____

_____

_____

_____

_____

_____

_____

_____

_____

_____

_____

_____

_____

_____

Skills used: _____

_____

_____

_____

_____

Interests: _____

_____

_____

_____

_____

_____

_____

Personality traits: _____

_____

_____

_____

_____

_____

_____

_____

_____

_____

_____

_____

Values: _____

_____

_____

_____

_____

Accomplishment #2: _____

_____

_____

_____

_____

_____

_____

_____

_____

_____

_____

_____

_____

_____

_____

_____

_____

_____

Skills used: _____

_____

_____

_____

_____

Interests: _____

_____

_____

_____

_____

_____

_____

Personality traits: _____

_____

_____

_____

_____

_____

_____

_____

_____

_____

_____

Values: _____

_____

_____

_____

_____

Repeat this worksheet as many times as you need to until you have written down 5 to 10 specific accomplishments.

9. 5 Guidelines for Vocational Testing

Vocational testing can be an excellent way to gather more information about your skills, interests, values, and personality style. Often, it helps clarify, organize, and confirm your thinking with regard to your best occupational choices.

Joseph Imburgia, president of Diagnostic Sciences, suggests the following guidelines be used to determine whether you are a good candidate for vocational testing.

	Yes	No
1. Are you the type of person who needs to have things spelled out in detail before you feel comfortable making a decision?	☐	☐
2. Do you have a difficult time expressing your career interests and your personal career strengths?	☐	☐
3. Do you feel that you are often too impulsive—that you are prone to make rash decisions?	☐	☐
4. Do you feel that your career interests and thinking fluctuate quite a bit—so much so that your career choices sometimes seem overwhelming or heavily ambivalent?	☐	☐
5. Do you feel that there is just too much information to handle effectively without having it organized in some way?	☐	☐

If you answer "yes" to any of the five questions, you should consider vocational testing.

10. 3 Types of Vocational Tests

Vocational testing can help you define your strengths, weaknesses, preferences, and style. Career counselors administer and interpret tests to help clarify, confirm, organize, and stimulate thinking with regard to career directions. There are three major types of tests you may want to consider:

1. **Interest inventories** measure your likes and dislikes, but they will not tell you whether you have any aptitude or ability in the areas that interest you. They will also compare your likes and dislikes to the interests of people who work in a wide variety of fields in order to determine whether there is a compatibility of interests.

The Strong Interest Inventory is one of the oldest and most highly respected interest tests available. The Career Assessment Inventory, the Kuder Occupational Interest Survey, and the Jackson Vocational Interest Survey are also quite popular.

2. **Aptitude tests** identify natural talents such as verbal, numerical, spatial, memory, reasoning, and clerical abilities. However, there are some good general tests that can highlight strengths and weaknesses, such as the GATB and the Employee Aptitude Survey.

3. **Personality Tests** help identify and measure specific personality traits. The Myers-Briggs Type Indicator is probably the most popular test. It uses a Jungian model to categorize people according to 16 personality types, including introversion-extroversion, sensing, feeling, judging, intuitive, and perceptive.

A complete battery of tests ranges from $150 to $600, with or without counseling. They are often administered through private testing services, university counseling centers, social service agencies, and private career counselors. If the price seems a little too steep, you might want to try your hand at Holland's Self-Directed Search. This self-administered and self-scored test combines ability and interest inventories and may be obtained for as little as $5 to $10 from many community resource centers. The drawback? Career tests may be difficult for novices to interpret without the help of a skilled counselor.

11. Brainstorming for Job Ideas

Although self-assessment is a continuous, lifelong process, it is important to tie that information into the job market in order to make effective career choice decisions. The following list is designed to increase your awareness of job possibilities. Circle those that interest you. If you are not familiar with a job title but would like to know more about it, put a question mark next to that particular title as a reminder to do some research. After you finish the list, examine the occupations that seem interesting to you. Do they have anything in common? Briefly jot down your conclusions in the *Occupations Summary* section at the end of the list.

Accountant
accounting clerk
activities therapist
actor
actuary
acupuncturist
administrative assistant
adult education instructor
advertising executive
agronomist
airline pilot
air traffic controller
anesthesiologist
animal health technician
animal trainer
announcer
antique dealer
anthropologist
appraiser
arborist
arbitrage clerk
archaeologist
architect
archivist
art appraiser
art dealer
art director
art teacher
art therapist
artificial intelligence
   specialist
astrologer

astronomer
athlete
athletic director
athletic trainer
auctioneer
audiologist
author
automobile mechanic

Babysitter
bacteriologist
baker
banker
barber
bartender
beautician/cosmetologist
belly dancer
biochemist
biologist
biology teacher
biomedical engineer
blood bank
   donor recruiter
boatbuilder
bodyguard
bookbinder
book editor
bookkeeper
botanist
brand manager
bricklayer

building contractor
building inspector
building manager
bus driver
business home economist
buyer

Cake decorator
career counselor
cardiologist
cardiology technician
cartographer
carpenter
cartoonist
caterer
cement mason
chauffeur
chef
chemical engineer
chemist
chemistry teacher
child care worker
child psychologist
chiropractor
chocolatier
choreographer
cinematographer
city manager
civil engineer
clown
college admissions officer

columnist
comedian
comedy writer
commercial artist
commodities trader
communications technician
community educator
community relations director
compliance officer
comptroller
computer graphics artist
computer operator
computer programmer
computer security specialist
conservationist
construction manager
construction worker
consultant
convention/
    conference planner
cook
copywriter
coroner
corporate fitness director
correction officer
costume designer
credit officer
critic
cross-cultural trainer
cruise director
curator
customer service
    representative

Dancer
dance teacher
dance therapist
data processing operator
data processing supervisor
day care director
dean
dental hygienist
dentist
design engineer
detective
development officer
diamond cutter
diesel mechanic
dietitian
dispatcher

diving instructor
dog groomer
dog trainer
drafter
drama coach
dressmaker
driver

Ecologist
economist
editor
educational psychologist
electrical engineer
electrician
electronics engineer
electronics technician
elementary school teacher
employee assistance
    counselor
employee benefits
    specialist
engraver
entertainer
environmental analyst
environmentalist
environmental lawyer
ergonomics engineer
estimator
evangelist
examiner
excavator
executive assistant
executive recruiter
executive secretary
exercise physiologist
exporter

Facilities planner
family life educator
family therapist
farmer
fashion designer
field representative
financial planner
firefighter
fish and game warden
fisher
fitness instructor
flight attendant

florist
food services
    supervisor
food scientist
foreign service officer
forensic psychologist
free-lance writer
fundraiser
furniture designer
furrier

Gambling dealer
gamekeeper
garbage collector
gardener
gemologist
genealogist
general contractor
general manager
geneticist
geographer
geologist
geriatric nurse
geriatric social worker
gerontologist
graphic artist
groundskeeper
gynecologist

Head coach
health care lawyer
health officer
health physicist
historian
history teacher
horse trainer
horticultural therapist
horticultural worker
hospice worker
hospital administrator
host
housekeeper
human resources
    representative
human resources director
hypnotist

Illustrator

image consultant
immigration attorney
importer
industrial hygienist
industrial social worker
information specialist
information systems
    consultant
inside sales representative
inspector
installer
instructor
insurance broker
interior designer
international meeting
planner
interpreter
interviewer
investigator

Jeweler
job placement counselor
journalist

Laboratory technician
labor relations representative
landscape architect
landscape contractor
law librarian
lawyer
legal assistant
librarian
linguist
literary agent
loan officer
lobbyist
lyricist

Machinist
magician
mail carrier
maintenance engineer
make-up artist
management trainee
management consultant
manager
manufacturer's representative
marine biologist

marine geologist
marketing assistant
marketing research director
masseur/masseuse
materials scientist
mathematician
mechanical engineer
media specialist
mediator
medical assistant
medical illustrator
medical photographer
medical records clerk
medical technologist
metallurgist
meteorologist
microbiologist
military officer
minister
model
mortician
mortuary beautician
motel/hotel manager
musician
music therapist

Naprapath
naturalist
navigator
nephrologist
newscaster
newspaper editor
newspaper publisher
newspaper reporter
newswriter
nurse
nurse-anesthetist
nurse-consultant
nurse-midwife
nurse's aide
nutritionist

Obstetrician
occupational analyst
occupational health and
    safety inspector
occupational therapist
oceanographer
office manager

operations manager
ophthalmologist
optician
optometrist
oral surgeon
organizational psychologist
ornithologist
orthoptist
orthotics assistant
osteopath
outplacement counselor
outreach worker

Painter
paleontologist
paperhanger
parachutist
paralegal
park ranger
parole officer
party planner
patient representative
pathologist
patternmaker
pawnbroker
payroll clerk
pediatric nurse
pediatrician
penologist
personal injury attorney
personal shopper
pharmacist
photographer
photojournalist
physician
physician assistant
physicist
podiatrist
poet
police officer
political scientist
politician
preschool teacher
priest
professor
program analyst
program director
proofreader
property manager
prosthetist

psychiatric aide
psychiatrist
psychologist
psychometrist
public affairs officer
public health educator
publicist
public relations representative
publisher
purchasing agent

Quality assurance
   control specialist

Rabbi
radiation biologist
radiographer
radiologic technologist
radio producer
reader
real estate developer
realtor
receptionist
recorder
recording engineer
recreational director
referee
registrar
rehabilitation therapist
repairer
reporter
research assistant
reservations agent
respiratory therapist
restaurant manager
restoration architect
retail salesperson
revenue officer
roboticist

Safety inspector
sales agent
salesperson
sales representative
sample maker
science teacher
science writer
scientist
scout
screenwriter
securities trader
security officer
seismologist
semiconductor development
   technician
set designer
shop steward
silversmith
skip tracer
social worker
sociologist
sound mixer
special events director
speech pathologist
speechwriter
statistician
stockbroker
store detective
storywriter
stripper
stunt person
substance abuse counselor
superintendent
supervisor
surveyor
systems analyst

Tailor
tattoo artist
tax analyst

tax attorney
technical writer
telemarketing representative
teller
theater manager
tour guide
tour operator
trainer
translator
travel agent
trucker
trust officer
typist

Ultrasound technologist
underwriter
urban planner
urologist
usher
utility worker

Veterinarian
veterinary technician
videotape recording engineer
volcanologist

Waiter
weather forecaster
wedding consultant
welder
wildlife agent
writer

X-ray technician

Youth counselor

Occupations Summary

_____

_____

_____

_____

_____

_____

_____

_____

_____

_____

_____

If there are occupations you would like to know more about, refer to the following reference books for more information:

Occupational Outlook Handbook, U.S. Government Department of Labor, published every two years.

Dictionary of Occupational Titles, U.S. Government Department of Labor, 1977.

VGM's Careers Encyclopedia, VGM Career Books, 1988.

12. 2 Forms of Career Research

Now that you have developed a target list of job possibilities, you need to learn more specifics. Basic job and career research usually takes two forms: published materials and informational interviews. First, let's explore the published market.

Published Materials

Libraries, bookstores, and professional associations are usually the best places to obtain written information related to any given field. In addition to the *Directory of Occupational Titles* and *VGM's Careers Encyclopedia*, you might want to check *Where to Start Career Planning*, compiled by the Cornell University Placement Center. This is a comprehensive bibliography of career resource books.

Informational Interviews

Informational interviews are the second key to career research. These interviews are a cornerstone to career change for two reasons. First, by talking with people who already work in the jobs or fields that interest you, you can learn better what that work is really like. This allows you to reality-test your ideas and clarify whether you are actually on the right track. Second, as a career changer, you probably lack networking contacts in your new areas of interest. Informational interviews are the beginning of a new network. Should you decide to pursue a job in that field, you already will have a built-in list of names of people who may be in a position to help you.

13. 4 Effective Steps for Doing Your Homework

Regardless of whether you are entering the work force for the first time, looking for a job, preparing for interviews, switching careers, starting a new business, or updating current knowledge, a day at the library can work wonders. The following four steps should help you use your library time more effectively.

1. Identify the library that best can serve your needs. To do this, you must determine as clearly as possible what kind of information you are seeking. For general career and job-hunting information, public and school libraries are usually your best bet.

    For more specific industry or occupational information, specialized libraries usually have the most comprehensive information. For example, if you are looking for information about the legal profession, a law school library makes the most sense. Or perhaps you have your own business and are looking for grant money? Try the Donors Forum Library. Say you are a psychologist who wants to see what's new in your field. The library at the Institute for Psychoanalysis might serve your needs well. Totally confused? Call the American Library Association first. The ALA staff can help you identify the library best suited to your needs.

2. Make sure that you are eligible for the library's services before making a trip to the facilities. Some special libraries limit their hours and user privileges. For example, some colleges and universities offer library services only to students, alumni, and employees. Others are open to the general public during restricted hours. Determine policies first, then you won't be disappointed later.

3. Make the librarian your ally. Take the librarian into your confidence. Explain your situation. Describe the kind of information you need. Ask for help. Perhaps the librarian can recommend reference books, directories, periodicals, or computer data bases that will yield the appropriate information. Don't be shy about asking questions. It's the librarian's job to help you.

4. Try not to be too myopic. Read some general information first. Having the big picture on an industry or organization gives a better understanding of the smaller picture as well.

14. 6 Good Ways to Review the Literature

1. Make friends with your local business librarian. Ask her or him to help you locate any directories related to your target fields, industries, or companies. The *Directory of Directories* will also prove useful in this regard.

2. Read newspapers, magazines, and trade journals for up-to-date information in your target areas.

3. Use the *Encyclopedia of Associations* to identify appropriate professional associations. Contact them for any printed literature or surveys. Ask about membership directories, job banks, newsletters, meetings, and conferences. Also, check to see whether they have an in-house professional library. These special libraries are usually the best source of information about a specific field.

4. Conduct a computer search for names of books and periodicals that relate to your area of interest.

5. Obtain a copy of *Where to Start Career Planning: Essential Resource Guide for Career Planning and Job Hunting* (Seventh Edition), compiled by Cornell University Career Center. This is a comprehensive, up-to-date bibliography of career information books.

6. Call or visit companies directly for any public relations materials, annual reports, newsletters, or other literature.

15. Literature Review Worksheets

Worksheet

Name of Field/Industry/Company: _____

_____

Source of Information: _____

Date/Author of Publication: _____

Notes: _____

_____

_____

_____

Source of Information: _____

Date/Author of Publication: _____

Notes: _____

_____

_____

_____

Source of Information: _____

Date/Author of Publication: _____

Notes: _____

_____

_____

_____

Source of Information: _____

Date/Author of Publication: _____

Notes: _____

_____

_____

_____

Source of Information: _____

Date/Author of Publication: _____

Notes: _____

_____

_____

_____

Worksheet #2

Name of Field/Industry/Company: _____

_____

Source of Information: _____

Date/Author of Publication: _____

Notes: _____

_____

_____

Source of Information: _____

Date/Author of Publication: _____

Notes: _____

_____

_____

_____

Source of Information: _____

Date/Author of Publication: _____

Notes: _____

_____

_____

_____

Source of Information: _____

Date/Author of Publication: _____

Notes: _____

_____

_____

_____

Source of Information: _____

Date/Author of Publication: _____

Notes: _____

_____

_____

_____

16. 5 Steps to Set Up an Informational Interview

1. Identify the career fields, industries, and organizations that you want to investigate further. Try to target areas that seem to match up most closely with your skills, interests, values, and personality style.

2. Ask people you know (relatives, acquaintances, friends, colleagues, past employers) if they can introduce you to someone who works there.

3. Use the *Encyclopedia of Associations* to identify professional groups in your target areas. If there is a local chapter, plan to attend one of its monthly meetings to make new contacts. Also, ask if there is a membership directory. You can use this list to target people who are appropriate contacts for informational interviews.

4. Once you have identified the people you want to meet, you can contact them by letter or telephone to schedule a convenient time to talk. During your initial contact, you must briefly tell them who you are, explain why you are contacting them, and ask for a short meeting. If they decline, ask if there is anyone else they can recommend that you call or write. If the answer is still "no," ask if they have any other ideas about how you might go about meeting people in their field.

5. Before the interview, plan a trip to the library. Read trade journals, annual reports, and other printed materials to glean as much information as possible in advance. Then you will be able to present yourself as a knowledgeable interviewee.

17. 26 Informational Interview Questions

The following questions are the type you will want to ask at an informational interview. You may want to write out a list to take with you, then take notes at the interview to help you remember the answers you were given.

1. How did you decide to work in this field? For this company?

2. What is a typical workday like? A typical week? Year?

3. Do you work under a lot of pressure? Is that expected?

4. How many hours per week do you usually work? Is it common to take work home?

5. Do you travel a lot?

6. Will you be expected to relocate?

7. Are there other responsibilities (such as civic or social obligations) that come with the territory?

8. What is the best training or education to acquire?

9. What was your background?

10. What skills do you typically use? Is there an opportunity to develop more skills or take on additional responsibilities?

11. Do you have an area of specialization? What?

12. How did you decide in which area to specialize? What are the other areas?

13. What are the most difficult problems/decisions/challenges you must face?

14. Is the field growing? What are the various types of employers?

15. How secure is employment?

16. Do your skills and experience translate well into self-employment opportunities?

17. Do you find that certain personality traits make it easier to do this work well? Which traits?

18. What is it like to work here?

19. What is the hiring process? Is that process standard procedure within the industry?

20. What is the best way to find a job?

21. If you could do it all over again, what would you do differently?

22. What is a typical starting salary?

23. Are there professional trade journals I should read? Which ones?

24. Do you belong to any professional associations? Can nonmembers attend meetings?

25. Would you mind reviewing my résumé and making comments or suggestions?

26. Can you recommend other people I might talk to?

18. Worksheet for Informational Interviews

Interview #1

Name of Contact: _____

Position: _____

Company/Organization: _____

Address: _____

Telephone: _____

Referral: _____

Method of contact: _____
   (letter or phone)

Date of first contact: _____

Purpose of interview: _____

Results: _____

_____

_____

_____

_____

_____

_____

_____

Follow-up: (Yes or No) _____

Date of follow-up: _____

Results: _____

_____

Interview #2

Name of Contact: _____

Position: _____

Company/Organization: _____

Address: _____

Telephone: _____

Referral: _____

Method of contact: _____

Date of first contact: _____

Purpose of interview: _____

Results: _____

_____

_____

_____

_____

_____

_____

_____

Follow-up: _____

Date of follow-up: _____

Results: _____

_____

Interview #3

Name of Contact: _____

Position: _____

Company/Organization: _____

Address: _____

Telephone: _____

Referral: _____

Method of contact: _____

Date of first contact: _____

Purpose of interview: _____

Results: _____

_____

_____

_____

_____

_____

_____

_____

Follow-up: _____

Date of follow-up: _____

Results: _____

_____

Interview #4

Name of Contact: _____

Position: _____

Company/Organization: _____

Address: _____

Telephone: _____

Referral: _____

Method of contact: _____

Date of first contact: _____

Purpose of interview: _____

Results: _____

_____

_____

_____

_____

_____

_____

_____

Follow-up: _____

Date of follow-up: _____

Results: _____

_____

Interview #5

Name of Contact: _____

Position: _____

Company/Organization: _____

Address: _____

Telephone: _____

Referral: _____

Method of contact: _____

Date of first contact: _____

Purpose of interview: _____

Results: _____

_____

_____

_____

_____

_____

_____

_____

_____

Follow-up: _____

Date of follow-up: _____

Results: _____

_____

_____

_____

Interview #6

Name of Contact: _____

Position: _____

Company/Organization: _____

Address: _____

Telephone: _____

Referral: _____

Method of contact: _____

Date of first contact: _____

Purpose of interview: _____

Results: _____

_____

_____

_____

_____

_____

_____

Follow-up: _____

Date of follow-up: _____

Results: _____

_____

19. The 9 Steps of Career Decision Making

Once you have stoked the fires of self-knowledge and increased your job-market awareness, you are in a better position to make career decisions. Career decision making is actually a process which can be learned if you develop good critical-thinking and problem-solving skills. The following 9 steps illustrate this process.

1. Define the problem.

2. Identify potential solutions.

3. Reality-test the options.

4. Review personal/professional values.

5. Make a preliminary decision.

6. Set goals.

7. Implement plan of action.

8. Review and revise goals.

9. Make final decision.

Example

Situation: Vickie is a fundraiser with a nonprofit organization. She would like to change jobs and possibly careers. Because her job consumes so much of her time, energy, and attention, she never has the time or energy to explore her options.

1. Define the problem. Vickie needs more time and energy to explore her job/career change options.

2. Identify potential solutions. (1) Quit her job without having another one. (2) Try to negotiate for part-time hours. (3) Take a temporary position. (4) Continue working full-time at her present job, but try to limit the amount of time and energy she devotes to the work.

3. Reality-test the options. (1) If she quits her job without having another one, she will need to support herself financially. After talking to her husband and reviewing their budget, they decide that they can realistically afford for her to be unemployed for three months. If Vickie looks for work within her current field, she may be able to find something within three months; however, she knows that a career change will take longer. (2) Looking over her job responsibilities, Vickie determines that part-time work is definitely out of the question. (3) After reviewing her marketable skills and talking with a few temporary employment agencies, Vickie believes that temporary jobs are a definite possibility. (4) After reviewing her schedule carefully, Vickie finds a few places where she could cut back hours; but she does not believe that she could cut back enough to effectively conduct a job search campaign.

4. Review personal/professional values. Vickie's values inventory indicates that she values creativity, independence, challenge, self-expression, helping others, and making a contribution to society. Therefore, it may be possible for her to change jobs without changing careers; but she would like to look at other fields which might also meet her needs.

5. Make a preliminary decision. Vickie decides to quit her job, in order to have enough time to properly make the job/career change decision.

6. Set goals. Vickie decides to devote three months of full-time effort to exploring her career change options while simultaneously looking for work in the same field. At the end of three months, she plans to have enough information to make the decision. If she has not found work by that time, she will sign up for temporary work.

7. Implement a plan of action. Vickie's plan of action begins by educating herself about the career choice and job search process. She visits a vocational counselor, takes vocational tests, reads job search books, writes her résumé, researches industries, and begins networking.

8. Review and revise goals. After exploring several career change options, Vickie realizes that she would need more education or training if she wanted to change fields. Since this alternative does not appeal to her, she elects to stay with her current career choice and look for a new job.

9. Make final decision. Change jobs within the same field.

20. Career Decision Making Worksheets

Decision No. 1

1. Define the problem. _____

   _____

   _____

   _____

2. Identify potential solutions. _____

   _____

   _____

   _____

   _____

   _____

   _____

3. Reality-test the options. _____

   _____

   _____

   _____

   _____

   _____

   _____

4. Review personal/professional values. _____

_____

_____

5. Make a preliminary decision. _____

_____

_____

6. Set goals. _____

_____

_____

7. Implement a plan of action. _____

_____

_____

_____

8. Review and revise goals. _____

_____

_____

9. Make a final decision. _____

_____

Decision No. 2

1. Define the problem. _____

_____

_____

_____

2. Identify potential solutions. _____

_____

_____

_____

_____

_____

3. Reality-test the options. _____

_____

_____

_____

_____

_____

4. Review personal/professional values. _____

_____

_____

5. Make a preliminary decision. _____

_____

_____

6. Set goals. _____

_____

_____

7. Implement a plan of action. _____

_____

_____

_____

8. Review and revise goals. _____

_____

_____

9. Make a final decision. _____

_____

Résumé and Cover Letter Smarts

"Not that the story need be long, but it will take a long while to make it short."

—Henry David Thoreau

21. 8 Building Blocks of a Good Résumé

Your résumé is *not* an autobiography. It is a self-marketing tool that encourages potential employers to want to know more about you. This means that you must selectively present information that demonstrates how and why you are qualified to work for your job objective. Although there is room for individual expression, most résumés include the following eight categories of information:

1. name, address, telephone number

2. job objective *or* summary statement

3. work history

4. skills and accomplishments

5. education

6. licenses and certificates

7. professional association memberships

8. awards

22. 22 Things Not to Include in Your Résumé

1. age

2. marital status

3. race

4. religion

5. height, weight, or other body measurements

6. photos

7. salary history or requirements

8. reasons you were fired or hostile comments about past jobs or former employers

9. personal pronouns ("I," "we," "you," "they")

10. names and addresses of references

11. jokes

12. spelling errors or typos

13. old addresses

14. disconnected telephone numbers or numbers where no one answers the telephone during the day

15. hobbies that are unrelated to job objective

16. white-out

17. black lines from the photocopy machine

18. illegible type

19. handwritten comments

20. coffee stains

21. erasures

22. jobs that lasted less than one month (unless you were hired on a time-limited basis)

> **HINT:** Take credit for your accomplishments, but don't overinflate them. An employer must trust that you are telling the truth. Otherwise, you will be eliminated from the competition.

23. Résumé Planner

Use this worksheet to assemble the information you will need for your résumé.

Work History

Working in reverse chronological order, describe your work history with your most recent employer.

Name of employer (company): _____

Address: _____

_____

Telephone: _____

Supervisor's name and title: _____

Job title: _____

Length/dates of service: _____

Responsibilities (use your job description, if necessary):

_____

_____

_____

Specific accomplishments: _____

_____

_____

_____

Skills used: _____

_____

_____

On-the-job training: _____

_____

Now do the same for your next-most-recent job. If necessary, copy this worksheet for any other previous jobs that lasted more than a month and are related to the position you are seeking.

Name of employer (company): _____

Address: _____

_____

Telephone: _____

Supervisor's name and title: _____

Job title: _____

Length/dates of service: _____

Responsibilities:

_____

_____

_____

Specific accomplishments: _____

_____

_____

_____

Skills used: _____

_____

_____

On-the-job training: _____

_____

Education

Name of college/university: _____

Location: _____

Dates attended: _____

Degree(s): _____

Major(s): _____

Minor(s): _____

Areas of concentration/related courses: _____

_____

_____

Internships/work-study programs: _____

_____

_____

Outside activities: _____

_____

_____

Special projects: _____

_____

Honors: _____

_____

_____

_____

Vocational education institution: _____

Location: _____

Dates Attended: _____

Program: _____

Certification: _____

Related coursework/training: _____

_____

_____

Skills: _____

_____

Internships: _____

_____

_____

_____

Honors: _____

_____

_____

Licenses and certificates _____

Name of granting institution or government: _____

_____

Title of license or certificate: _____

Date received: _____

Name of granting institution or government: _____

_____

Title of license or certificate: _____

Date received: _____

Professional Association Memberships

Name of organization: _____

Dates of membership: _____

Offices held: _____

Activities: _____

Accomplishments: _____

Name of organization: _____

Dates of membership: _____

Offices held: _____

Activities: _____

Accomplishments: _____

Awards

Title of award: _____

Date received: _____

Purpose of award: _____

Name of granting organization: _____

Relevant Volunteer Activities

Name of organization: _____

Dates: _____

Titles or offices held: _____

Activities: _____

Accomplishments: _____

24. 6 Exercises to Help You Establish Your Objective

Your résumé is a self-marketing tool. It is your calling card, your passport to job interviews. Therefore, it is very important that you present your qualifications in a way that will convince employers to interview you. Having an objective is extremely important because it makes a convincing argument that you are a person with goals and direction. Employers like that characteristic in an employee.

Your objective is a statement of what you can, will, and want to do for them. While objectives are not cast in concrete—you may have several résumés with a different objective on each one—they do provide an excellent way for you to organize the information you wish to present.

Example: I would like to use my technical skills and education in the field of computer programming.

If you do not know the specific job title, you can state your objective by describing your preferred environment and skills.

Example: I would like to use my research, communication, and interpersonal skills in a social service agency.

The body of the résumé should go on to describe why you are qualified for this type of position. Everything that follows should keep your objective in mind—from the format you select, to the language you choose, to the information you include. Even if you are not sure exactly what you are looking for, you can use the objective as a way of organizing your job search. It will create an illusion of self-direction that will allow you to negotiate your way through the job market effectively. While you are honing your job-hunting skills, you will also be acquiring information and confidence in your marketability that will allow you to further develop and refine your objective later.

The following exercises will help you establish your first objective.

1. If you already know what you are looking for, write it down here. Otherwise, leave this section blank.

    _____

    _____

2. Review your skills inventory. What skills have you acquired through

work, education, or extracurricular activities that you particularly enjoy using?

_____

_____

3. Review your interest inventory. List your strongest interests on the lines below.

_____

_____

4. You have also completed an exercise on working conditions. List your preferences here.

_____

_____

5. Now describe your ideal job. What skills will you be using? What setting will you be working in? Will you be working alone or as part of a team? Indoors or outside? Large organization or small? Lots of freedom? Highly structured? Be as specific as possible.

_____

_____

_____

6. If you are still not sure, go back to the résumé planner in the previous section to help organize your thinking further.

_____

_____

_____

_____

> **HINT:** If you are unsure of your objective, use a summary instead. You can put your job objective in the cover letter when you know the name and type of position you are applying for.

25. Selecting the Right Résumé Format: 6 Basic Types

A résumé is a marketing tool. Its purpose is to help you get an interview. Therefore, it should represent the best possible presentation of your experience and skill.

There is no such thing as a perfect résumé. There are many different formats and styles from which to choose. Since certain types of résumés work best for specific situations, it is important to educate yourself about your options. Six basic résumé types are detailed in the paragraphs that follow.

1. *Chronological résumés* present your work history in reverse chronological order, starting with your most recent experience. This is the most widely accepted résumé format, because it usually survives the "skim test." That means an employer can quickly review your work history and responsibilities and determine if further action is required.

   This may have pros and cons attached to it. If you are not a job-hopper, do not suffer from employment gaps, and can show steady, upward career progression, this format usually is a safe bet. On the other hand, if you cannot show upward movement, have changed careers, switched jobs several times, or missed lengthy amounts of time between jobs, this format will highlight those perceived deficits a little too clearly. Also, if you are new to the workplace and have little experience, a format that emphasizes work history will not show your skills to their best advantage.

2. *Functional résumés*, also sometimes referred to as *skill-based résumés*, place the emphasis on what you can do, rather than where you have done it. Although some employers may frown suspiciously upon functional résumé users, this format does have a few distinct advantages. First, it allows you to deemphasize your employment history and focus on your skills. Second, it allows you to group your skills together in a meaningful way regardless of where those skills were acquired. That provides an ideal opportunity to incorporate skills and experiences acquired through volunteer activities and hobbies. When done properly, a functional résumé also can survive that all-important skim test.

3. *Targeted résumés* are written for specific job openings. If you have your résumé on a word processor, it should not be too difficult to tailor your objective, language, and accomplishments toward individual positions or companies. Some job hunters have a standard résumé boilerplate with individual inserts that they can use, depending on the nature of the position for which they are applying.

4. *Letter résumés* transpose the information from your standard résumé

into business letter format. This style works best when you are initiating contact with an employer who has not advertised an open position. The assumption is that employers who are not hiring tend to ignore résumés, whereas personalized letters (even from job hunters) are more likely to get read.

5. *Curriculum Vitae* are résumés that are used to apply for academic jobs or professional positions in academia. They are usually longer than traditional résumés because employers want to see a complete list of grants, research projects, and publications.

6. *Portfolios* are visual résumés used by people in creative or artistic fields to showcase their work. They are often oversized leatherbound or plastic briefcases containing pictures, photographs, articles, illustrations, and other creative products. Portfolios are usually accompanied by some printed information.

And now, a pop quiz!

1. You have worked for one company for the last eight years. You started out in a clerical position and gradually worked your way up into middle management. What format works best for your situation?

_____

2. After eight years working for the same employer in progressively responsible positions, you have decided that you want to make a career change. Your preferred résumé format?

_____

3. Through no fault of your own, you have been forced to change jobs three times in the last five years. Fortunately, you have always landed on your feet, but you think employers might perceive you as a job-hopper. Your résumé format?

_____

4. You are a new graduate, looking for your first professional job. What format should you use?

_____

5. You have been home with your kids for the last six years, but you have not been idle. You have been managing your household. You have also been very active in local politics, church, and school activities. How should you present your experience?

_____

6. You are a research chemist for a large university. Recently, the funding ran out on your grant. You have decided to look for a position in the private sector, possibly with a chemical or scientific instruments company. Your résumé?

_____

7. You are a history professor who was denied tenure. You want to look for another job in academia. Your résumé format?

_____

8. You are a secretary who wants to get into the field of public relations. You have been doing lots of volunteer work for community organizations in order to get more public relations experience. Your format?

_____

9. You are a computer programmer with a stable work history. You have changed jobs twice in the last 10 years. Although your job responsibilities have always been basically the same, you have always increased your earning potential significantly. You are ready to change jobs again. Your format?

_____

Answer key:

1. Chronological. You can show steady, upward professional development and a solid employment history.

2. Your job objective is the key here. Use a functional résumé to highlight your transferable skills. Otherwise, employers will tend to slot you into a position that does not meet your current objectives.

3. Functional résumés deemphasize employment history.

4. Functional résumés highlight skills. Since you have not yet established a strong work history, you need a format that can integrate some of your other experiences and skills.

5. Again, a functional résumé will work better.

6. If you are looking for a research chemist position, you can use a chronological résumé that has been targeted for private industry. Your clearly stated job objective will be an important key here. To increase the sense of a good fit, emphasize budget management responsibilities. Quantify your accomplishments, whenever possible.

7. Curriculum vitae is the preferred format.

8. A portfolio will provide evidence of your accomplishments. You might also want to attach a functional résumé highlighting skills and accomplishments.

9. You have a hard decision. A chronological will illustrate your stable work history and be more popular with traditional employers. However, you may run the risk of repetition. Try to vary your language so that employers will not become bored with your work history and abandon you.

> **HINT:** In designing your résumé, try not to be too rigid about the one-page rule. If the breadth and depth of your experience can be better expressed through a two-page format, go for it! Most employers would rather see a little more information about you than rely too heavily on some arbitrary notion that every résumé should be confined to one page.

26. 4 Sample Résumés

Chronological

GEORGE R. SAMUELS
59 W. Main Street
Elkhart, IN 86440
(219) 555-6554

SUMMARY	More than 8 years of management experience. Broadbased background in business development, operations management, purchasing, inventory control, personnel, training, promotions, and customer service/relations.
	Solid research, organizational, writing, and interpersonal skills.
PROFESSIONAL EXPERIENCE 1985– present	*Manager,* RJR Enterprises, Inc., Elkhart, IN
	Successfully restructured and developed an existing restaurant into a thriving, contemporary operation.
	—Increased revenues by 250% in first year
	—Redesigned physical facility to improve efficiency and comfort
	Designed and delivered employee training program to professional operations.
	Recruited, supervised, and evaluated staff.
	Planned and coordinated advertising and direct mail campaigns and promotional events.
	—Created and implemented a unique New Year's Eve package that was copied by competitors.
1980– 1985	*Assistant Manager,* Bob's Restaurant, Lee, IN
	Managed night operations for restaurant.
	Hired, trained, and supervised support staff.
	Monitored operations and service to ensure efficiency and customer satisfaction.
	Resolved customer complaints; promoted goodwill.
	Implemented nightly closing procedures.
EDUCATION	B.S., Business Administration University of Indiana, Indianapolis, 1982
	A.A., Hospitality Management Triton College, River Grove, Illinois, 1980
MEMBERSHIP	National Restaurant Association

Chronological

JOHN CENTER
299 Columbia Street
New York, NY 07041
Home: (201) 555-6599   Work: (201) 555-1000

OBJECTIVE: Senior financial management position utilizing accounting, auditing, and administrative skills.

EXPERIENCE: *Accountant,* Fox & Wentworth, New York, 1979–present

Responsible for managing the firm's audit department.

Supervise audit engagements of publicly and privately owned companies. Client industries include: manufacturing, insurance, retail, and health care companies.

Recruit, train, supervise, and evaluate support personnel.

Wrote company booklet describing practices and philosophy of audit department.

Prepare and present practice development programs at professional meetings.

Auditor, Smith, Klein & Smith, New York, 1975–1979

Audited financial records for health care and pharmaceutical company clients.

EDUCATION   B.S., Accounting, City Colleges of New York, 1975

CERTIFICATE   Certified Public Accountant, 1979

MEMBERSHIPS   American Institute of Certified Public Accountants

Society of CPAs, New York Chapter

EDITH MARTIN
2450 N. Rice Avenue
Houston, TX 77440
(713) 555-9856

Objective: Position in training and development writing and producing audiovisual materials

EDUCATION

M.A., Instructional Design, University of Houston, 1987
B.A., Education, Texas State University, 1982
   Student Internship: Northwest High School, Houston

PROFESSIONAL ACHIEVEMENTS

Training/Teaching
- ☐ Developed and facilitated skills training for youth.
- ☐ Designed and delivered personal growth and motivation seminars for professional groups.
- ☐ Taught English grammar and composition to ninth and tenth grade students.
- ☐ Participated in Curriculum Development Committee.

Production
- ☐ Produced a slide/cassette presentation for a community college for recruitment purposes.
- ☐ Served as production assistant for cable TV station.

Writing
- ☐ Wrote restaurant reviews and personality profiles that were published in central Texas publications.
- ☐ Wrote feature articles to promote enrollment in community college seminars.

EMPLOYMENT HISTORY

1987–present   *Recruitment Coordinator*
             Central Texas Community College, Houston, TX

1982–1985   *English Teacher*
             Houston Public School System, Houston, TX

CERTIFICATES

Type 9 Certificate, National Collegiate Association for Teacher Education, 1982.

PROFESSIONAL ASSOCIATIONS

Member, American Society for Training and Development

Functional

DEBORAH L. JACOBS
850 N. State Street, #27K
Chicago, IL 60610
(312) 555-1535

PROFILE

Established counselor, administrator, educator, and author with strong national and local reputation. Knowledgeable in career development, business management, and vocational psychology. Excellent organizational, interpersonal, and communication skills.

COUNSELOR

Counsel adults on career choice/change, planning, development, management, and job search issues.

Consult to corporations, government agencies, schools, and professional associations. Clients include: AT&T, Robert Morris College, Chicago Bar Association. Currently administer regional counseling program for Nuclear Regulatory Commission.

ADMINISTRATOR

Design and implement public and community relations programs to promote private practice. Media relations efforts resulted in appearances on CBS, WGN, WFYR, and WBEZ.

Supervised neighborhood development programs for the elderly, including: outreach, advocacy, peer and staff counseling.

Managed 50-person corporate law firm. Responsible for facilities management, human resources, and general administration. Coordinated relocation efforts, purchase and installation of telephone and computer systems.

EDUCATOR

Design and teach courses in "The Future American Workplace" and "Career Development" at DePaul University. Advise students.

Present workshops and seminars on career development and job search topics to professional associations and continuing education programs. Clients include: American Marketing Association, Chicago Women in Publishing, Discovery Center, Latin School, and National Association of Bank Women.

(Continued)

AUTHOR

Write magazine and newspaper articles on career development and job search topics. Currently author of "ShopTalk," a weekly career advice column published by the *Chicagoland Job Source.* Articles have also appeared in *Business Week Careers* and *National Business Employment Weekly.*

EMPLOYMENT HISTORY

1984–present	Career Counselor/Psychotherapist Private Practice, Chicago
1983–1984	Supervisor of Neighborhood Development Council for Jewish Elderly, Chicago
1976–1981	Office Manager Panter, Nelson & Bernfield, Ltd., Chicago

EDUCATION

Northwestern University, Evanston, IL
M.A., Counseling Psychology, 1983

Externship: Catholic Charities, Family Counseling Center
Practicum: Jewish Vocational Service

University of Iowa, Iowa City, IA
B.A., English/Secondary Education, 1973

Internship: West High School, Iowa City (10th grade English)

AWARDS

Community Leaders in America
Dictionary of International Biography
International Directory of Distinguished Leadership
International Who's Who of Intellectuals
International Who's Who of Business and Professional Women
Outstanding Young Women in America
Who's Who of Emerging Leaders in America
Who's Who in the Midwest
World Who's Who of Women
2,000 Notable American Women
5,000 Personalities of the World

PROFESSIONAL ASSOCIATIONS

American Psychological Association
Association of Labor-Management Consultants on Alcoholism to Industry (ALMACA)
American Orthopsychiatric Association

27. 8 Steps toward Verbalizing Your Accomplishments

Regardless of the résumé format you choose to use, every résumé must demonstrate your skills and accomplishments clearly. This is one of the hardest parts of résumé construction, so be patient with yourself. It's going to take a little practice.

1. Start by writing one-line statements about various aspects of employment and volunteer experience. Use the worksheets you created in the process of establishing your job objective to organize your thoughts.

2. Take each job or activity and write one-line statements describing various aspects of your experience. Starting with an action word, describe what you actually did and/or accomplished as a result of your action.

3. Brainstorm for ideas. Include everything now without making any editorial decisions. Your goal is to create a long list of one-line phrases.

Examples: Resolved customer complaints and problems
Supervised a team of clerical workers
Recruited, screened, and interviewed job prospects
Conducted a telephone survey
Prepared payroll information
Sold vacuum cleaners
Typed letters and other correspondence
Responded to telephone calls and questions

4. Once you have your basic ideas in place, quantify your experience appropriately.

Examples: Supervised a 12-person clerical staff
Prepared and managed a $25,000 budget
Coordinated a caseload of 50 clients
Generated $50,000 in sales
Covered a 6-state territory
Interviewed, hired, and trained 15 bartenders and waitresses

5. Show results, whenever possible.

Examples: Created and implemented customer service training program that resulted in improved customer satisfaction.
Developed cold call strategy which increased sales by 50 percent.
Initiated a public relations strategy that significantly increased visibility.

Note: Not all accomplishments are quantifiable, but most actions do have results. When you can identify and state those results clearly, this will demonstrate that you are a results-oriented person.

6. When you have completed this exercise for each of your jobs and/or activities, go back and edit. Review each statement to determine whether a reader can easily visualize what you did and how you did it. If the picture looks muddy, keep trying. Also, ask a professional counselor, trusted friend, or close relative to critique your work and make suggestions for improvement.

7. People who are using a chronological résumé format should list their one-line statements directly under the place where they acquired their experience. For those who are using a functional résumé, there is an additional step.

8. Functional résumé users need to group their one-liners into skill groups. Go through each of your statements and assign a letter "A," "B," "C," or "D" next to each of the major skill areas that you have identified as relevant in your job objective. The sample résumés illustrate how this works.

Bravo! The hardest part of your résumé is done.

28. Adding Verbs to Your Résumé

Verbs help employers picture you in action. The following list has been developed to stimulate your imagination. Circle the verbs that best describe your activities, and use them in your résumé.

advise	finalize	persuade
analyze	forecast	plan
assess	formulate	prepare
build	handle	promote
calculate	identify	purchase
chart	implement	recruit
communicate	influence	regulate
compile	initiate	represent
conceptualize	integrate	research
coordinate	interpret	sell
create	interview	service
cultivate	itemize	solve
decide	maintain	strengthen
delegate	manage	supervise
design	measure	teach
diagnose	modify	train
direct	motivate	unify
draft	negotiate	utilize
edit	organize	verify
enforce	penetrate	write
evaluate	perform	

29. 10 Tips for Punctuating Your Résumé

1. Use sentence fragments rather than complete sentences.

2. Skip the 'I' pronoun and begin statement with verbs. Since your name is at the top of the page, it is assumed that you are talking about your own experience and accomplishments.

3. Use semicolons to separate independent clauses that are not joined by conjunctions.

4. Put periods at the end of complete thoughts.

5. Use a colon to illustrate that the examples or details which follow expand the preceding phrase. *Example:* Clients include: AT&T, Chicago Bar Association, Nuclear Regulatory Commission.

6. Avoid brackets.

7. Capitalize words in major section headings.

8. Capitalize major words in the names and titles of books, articles, and presentations.

9. When in doubt, consult a style manual such as *The Chicago Manual of Style,* published by the University of Chicago Press. Your school or public librarian can help you identify an appropriate resource tool.

10. In some circumstances, you may want to use punctuation in an unusual way. If you choose to do so, at least be consistent.

30. 7 Ways to Make Your Education Count

The education section of your résumé is extremely important. How and what you choose to emphasize depends on your individual circumstances and job objective. The following situations illustrate how you can better think about your presentation.

1. If you are a new graduate with limited work experience, put your education right underneath your job objective. Play it up by including a list of internships, related coursework, and extracurricular activities.

2. Career changers with new degrees may also want to put education credentials right up front. This will demonstrate your commitment and credentials to enter this new area.

3. On the other hand, career changers who are hoping to capitalize on transferable skills will want to put the education section toward the rear.

4. If you received your degree a few years back but have been working in unrelated areas, your job objective will determine where you place your education. If you still want to get into the field, put your education first. If your job objective is to capitalize on your recent work experiences rather than your education, place your education behind your work history and accomplishments.

5. If your degree is more than five years old and you have been working in a related field, put your education behind your experience.

6. Every rule is meant to be broken. If you went to a very prestigious school whose name impresses people, you may want to put that information up front because it will immediately establish your credibility.

7. If you are an academic, *always* put your education first.

31. 11 Hints About References

1. Make sure your references have given you permission to use their names.

2. Names, addresses, and telephone numbers of references should never be included on your résumé.

3. References should never be supplied prior to a personal interview, regardless of how insistent a potential employer might be.

4. After you have interviewed for a position, give some thought as to which people might be the most appropriate references for that particular situation.

5. *Each time* you give an employer the name of one of your references, telephone your reference to advise him or her that someone will be calling to discuss your qualifications. Give the details of the job description and the nature of your discussions with the company. If there are any particular areas of skill or experience you would like your reference to mention, don't be shy about saying what you want and need. Someone who volunteers to be your reference usually has a genuine interest in helping you. Capitalize on that knowledge.

6. Protect your references from overuse. Unless you are genuinely interested in a position and an employer is genuinely interested in you, don't waste everyone's time. Your references will appreciate your courtesy.

7. You are not obligated to use your former supervisors as references if you feel that they will not be complimentary to you. Find the people who can honestly attest to your capabilities without reservation. Perhaps someone from another department who worked with you can speak favorably and knowledgeably about your skills; also, consider former clients and coworkers as possible references.

8. If you are unsure what a reference will say, call and ask first. Then, if you are uncomfortable with the comments, don't use that person as a reference.

9. If you sense that a person who has volunteered to be a reference is not helping your cause, consider using a reference checking service to get a better feel for what information is being conveyed.

10. Written references also can be useful. They should always be written on company letterhead for authenticity. Also, ask the author to be as specific as possible about your skills and accomplishments.

11. Keep track of your references. In today's mobile society, people move from one job to another quite often. Make sure that you know where that person has gone. Otherwise, you may find a few years down the road nobody left in a company knows or remembers your work.

> **HINT:** By law, employers are not allowed to say anything that will prevent you from obtaining new work. If you suspect that a past employer is badmouthing you to prospective employers, you may want to seek legal remedies.

32. Reference Worksheet

Name of reference: _____

Address: _____

_____

Telephone number(s): _____

Current employer: _____

Position: _____

Nature of previous relationship: _____

_____

Agreed to serve as a reference: _____

Date of contact: _____

Discussion notes: _____

_____

_____

Follow-up: _____

_____

Name of reference: _____

Address: _____

_____

Telephone number(s): _____

Current employer: _____

Position: _____

Nature of previous relationship: _____

_____

Agreed to serve as a reference: _____

Date of contact: _____

Discussion notes: _____

_____

_____

Follow-up: _____

_____

HINT: Protect your references. Don't give their names out unless you are sure an employer is genuinely interested in hiring you. Otherwise, they may begin to resent the intrusion upon their time.

HINT: If you cannot use your current supervisor as a reference (because you are still employed), try to find someone else you trust within the organization who can vouch for your work record.

33. 7 Guidelines for Résumé "Art"

Treat your résumé like it is a work of art that you are creating for a particular audience. It must be aesthetically pleasing and well-crafted.

1. Pretend your paper is your canvas. Invest in good quality bond. Use conservative colors: white, ivory, pale gray. You don't want the paper to overwhelm or outshine the content.

2. Respect your reader. Type should be crisp and clear. Word processors and typesetters are excellent; a high-quality typewriter is good. Dot-matrix printers are terrible. If employers find it hard to read, they will never get far enough to buy what you have to sell.

3. Organize your thoughts and presentation. Select a format that showcases your skills and experience most effectively.

4. Sketch a picture of your ideal self in action. Use verbs to create a sense of movement. Adjectives (in moderation) add spice to the picture.

5. Edit your work. This is not "true confessions." The impulse to "the truth, the whole truth, and nothing but the truth" belongs in a court of law, not a job search strategy. Do not lie, but you may omit details that might cast you in an unflattering light.

6. Be precise. Quantify your experiences and accomplishments for better comprehension and effect.

7. Remember the finishing touches. They reflect your attention to detail. Proofread carefully for mistakes. Eliminate ragged margins, dense copy, and other imperfections. Your résumé should be a reflection of your very best self.

34. Résumé Summary Worksheet

Now that your résumé is complete, check it over to make sure that it is your best possible effort. Are all of the following elements included?

☐ Name, address, telephone number(s)

☐ Job objective(s)

☐ Education
_____ Name of institution
_____ Dates attended
_____ Areas of concentration/major
_____ Related coursework (if appropriate)
_____ School activities, memberships

☐ Work History
_____ Name of employer
_____ Location
_____ Dates of employment
_____ Job title
_____ Responsibilities
_____ Accomplishments

☐ Other experiences that demonstrate skills, interests, and experiences
_____ Volunteer activities
_____ Hobbies

☐ Awards and scholarships
☐ Licenses and certifications

☐ I know why I have included each piece of information.
☐ My résumé is targeted toward my objective.
☐ The language is concise and action-oriented.
☐ I have proofread for errors.
☐ My résumé looks professional and easy-to-read.

35. 8 Rules for Writing a Cover Letter

To write an effective—and concise—cover letter, follow these eight rules. After you've finished your letter, read the list again and check to make sure you've followed each rule.

☐ 1. Always address the letter to a specific person by name and title. You usually can obtain that information from the company's switchboard operator or a department secretary.

☐ 2. Introduce yourself in the first paragraph. Tell the reader how you know about the company and why you are writing.

☐ 3. Elaborate briefly upon your qualifications in the second paragraph, stating why you are qualified to work for this firm. If you have a significant accomplishment you would like to mention, this is the time and place to do it. If your work history is extensive, you may want to take two paragraphs to explain a little about yourself—but don't go overboard.

☐ 4. Refer the reader to your résumé for more information.

☐ 5. Ask for an interview.

☐ 6. Tell the reader how to contact you.

☐ 7. Say thank-you.

☐ 8. Sign off nicely, typically with "Sincerely" or "Yours truly."

36. 10 Ways to Wreck a Cover Letter

1. Spell the name of the company incorrectly.

2. Send the letter to the wrong address.

3. Send the letter to the personnel department or company president without getting the exact name and title of the person you are contacting.

4. Address the letter "Dear Sir:" even when the hiring authority is a woman.

5. Misspell words; make typographical errors.

6. Use wrinkled-up paper (for effect).

7. Use poor grammar.

8. Forget to enclose your résumé.

9. Leave out your telephone number. Better yet, provide one where no one is home during the day. Then, if someone tries to call you, you won't be there.

10. Tell them you will follow up, then wait for them to call you.

37. Cover Letter Worksheet

Hiring authority: _____

Company name: _____

Address: _____

_____

Greeting: _____

Why you are writing: _____

_____

_____

Describe your qualifications. _____

_____

_____

_____

_____

More qualifications:_____

_____

_____

Enclose your résumé. _____

Ask for an interview. _____

Say thank-you. _____

Sign-off. _____

Hiring authority: _____

Company name: _____

Address: _____

_____

Greeting: _____

Why you are writing: _____

_____

_____

Describe your qualifications. _____

_____

_____

_____

_____

More qualifications: _____

_____

_____

Enclose your résumé. _____

Ask for an interview. _____

Say thank-you. _____

Sign-off. _____

38. 2 Sample Cover Letters

Sample #1

1050 N. State Street
Chicago, IL 60611

October 30, 199–

Ms. Jane Smith
Director of Communications
Windy City Hospital
One Hospital Drive
Oak Brook, IL 60023

Dear Ms. Smith:

While working as a public relations representative at a local hospital association, I learned that Windy City Hospital has developed a reputation for its innovative, high-quality services and programs. I am contacting you to determine whether you might have a need for an experienced public relations professional with a knowledge of the medical field.

For the last five years, I have been extensively involved in media relations and have developed excellent media contacts. I also have written articles on a variety of topics, which were published in professional trade journals and newsletters. The enclosed résumé will describe my qualifications in greater detail.

I would appreciate the opportunity to meet with you to discuss the possibility of working together. I will call you next week to arrange a convenient meeting time. In the meantime, please feel free to contact me at (312) 555-3000 if you would like to talk further.

Thank you for your interest. I look forward to speaking with you.

Sincerely,

David Jones

Enclosure

Sample #2

875 W. Belmont
Chicago, IL 60657

November 30, 199–

Ms. Sheila James
Director of Sales
Widget Manufacturers of America
6000 Hardware Plaza
Oakbrook, IL 60022

Dear Ms. James:

Your advertisement in the *Chicago Tribune* for a Sales Associate indicated that you currently are looking for an experienced sales representative.

For the last five years, I have been selling appliances for Sears, Roebuck & Co. I have a reputation for being a very customer service-oriented sales representative who goes out of her way to resolve customer complaints. As a result, I have established a loyal base of customers who seek my assistance when they have questions or concerns. At this time, I am interested in transferring my sales abilities to an outside sales position where I will be able to use my initiative, communication, and problem-solving skills effectively.

The position that was advertised sounds well-suited to my needs and qualifications. Certainly, I would appreciate the opportunity to interview with you to learn more about it. I can be reached during the day at 555-0976 or evenings at 555-0912.

Thank you for your interest. I look forward to hearing from you.

Sincerely,

Wanda Washington

Job-Search Strategies and Techniques

"Society is held together by communication and information."

—James Boswell

39. When Is it Time to Quit Your Job? An 11-Point Checklist

We are witnessing the evolution of a new work ethic which prizes both success and satisfaction. When people have financial success and job security, they get locked into a syndrome that is sometimes referred to as "golden handcuffs." On the other hand, bailing out at the first sign of trouble is merely running away. To discover the proper balance, determine how many of the following situations apply to you. When you have completed the checklist, the next section will focus on ways that you can transform your situation into a happier one.

Checklist

- [ ] 1. I have mastered my job. The work is no longer challenging.

- [ ] 2. I have no control over my work. My days are too stressful.

- [ ] 3. I don't get along with my boss.

- [ ] 4. I don't like my coworkers.

- [ ] 5. I feel like I don't fit in.

- [ ] 6. I don't like the way my organization does business.

- [ ] 7. I feel like I don't really have a career path. There's nowhere else to go.

- [ ] 8. My job performance is only so-so.

- [ ] 9. I don't make enough money.

- [ ] 10. There is not enough job security for me.

- [ ] 11. The hours are too long. I want more time for other things, like family and friends.

Responses

1. The opportunity to grow and learn new things is an important piece of your career development. Experts estimate that it takes approximately two to five years to master most jobs; after that, new challenges often are necessary. You have a few options available to you. First, you can make a lateral move within your organization, to stimulate new learning. Sec-

ond, you can volunteer to take on new projects or responsibilities. Third, you can move on to new organizations. Before making this decision, evaluate your current situation closely to determine whether there are ways to grow within your company; if not, consider moving on.

2. Determine whether the lack of control is related to the nature of the work itself, poor company or department organization, or your personal working style. If the problem is related to the work itself, perhaps only a change of career will remedy the situation. For company or departmental disorganization, you can initiate discussions with your employer or take the initiative to bring more organization to the work. If this proves impossible, you can try setting limits. Determine what you can and cannot realistically do. Don't beat yourself up if you haven't managed to conquer the unconquerable. Or, if you prefer, you can move on to a better-managed organization. If the problem lies within your personal work style, you will need to develop better organizational skills. In this latter case, no amount of moving around will resolve the conflict. It must be tackled from the inside.

3. Try to determine whether the problem is related to a personality clash, a power struggle, or both. If you are involved in a power struggle, you will undoubtedly lose. In this case, back off or get out. Personality clashes can be equally devastating. Try to determine whether there is a better way you can relate to this person to make your work lives together more enjoyable. However, if it seems impossible, request a transfer to another department—or plan to move on to another company as quickly as possible.

4. You are under no obligation to love your coworkers. However, your work life will be a lot more pleasant if you can work cooperatively and professionally together. Of course, if you are someone who wants and needs to create a social life around the work life, you may feel extremely frustrated with this situation. To assess the importance of this factor, refer back to Checklist 3, "15 Work-Related Values." Review your priorities and make your decision accordingly.

5. Not fitting in with the culture can be a painful experience. If you find that your values and personality clash with the organizational culture, it may be hard to be successful in that environment. In that case, look for a better match.

6. Say goodbye.

7. First, evaluate your career priorities. How important is upward mobility? Can you initiate new projects that will lead to new responsibilities? Have you initiated discussions with your boss expressing your concerns? If neither of these efforts bring results, start looking around for another place to work.

8. Determine the reasons why. Perhaps the work itself is not a good match for your interests or skills. Are you unmotivated by the work? Perhaps a

clash of values is the culprit. Do you feel your employer doesn't appreciate you? Figuring out the reasons why should pinpoint ways to resolve the conflict.

9. What is the salary range for your job? Have you reached the top of that range? If you are at the top of your range—and that range is consistent with industry standards—you probably need a career change more than a job change.

10. If you fear that your job is in jeopardy, activate the pieces of your job search immediately. However, keep in mind that job security in today's workplace is largely a luxury of the past. Build *career* security with a good foundation of skills, including solid job-search skills.

11. Is the pressure to work long hours coming from you or your boss? Do you feel driven to succeed? Perhaps the problem is a psychological one that will remain with you wherever you go. However, if it is coming from the environment, you may want to look around for a job with a better values and life-style match.

40. 8 Ways to Breathe Life into a Boring Job

1. Volunteer for new projects or assignments.

2. Rewrite your job description.

3. Get promoted.

4. Apply for lateral positions.

5. Sign up for company training programs.

6. Enroll in night school or weekend classes.

7. Negotiate a leave of absence.

8. Take your career elsewhere—find a new job.

41. Help! I've Been Fired!

Losing your job, whether through firing or layoff, can be a traumatic experience. Try not to ignore or cover up your feelings. By recognizing your worst fears and fantasies, you will be able to place them in perspective—and get on with the business of creating new opportunities. From the list below, check off the statements that reflect your fears. Then continue reading in this chapter to learn how to deal with these feelings and conduct a successful job search.

☐ No one will hire me.

☐ I will have to take a pay cut.

☐ I am too old to find a new job.

☐ My family will leave me.

☐ There must be something wrong with me.

☐ I must have done something wrong.

☐ My skills are obsolete.

☐ Everyone will know I didn't get along with my boss or coworkers.

☐ My former employer will badmouth me.

☐ I can't afford to make another mistake.

☐ Other: _____

HINT: People who are unemployed today may be employed tomorrow—and vice versa. Don't burn your bridges behind you by making too many enemies. Those people may be in a position to hire or fire you in the future.

42. 4 Steps Toward Recovery From Firing or Layoff

1. Acknowledge your feelings. When you get fired or laid off from a position, you will often find yourself filled with conflicting feelings: anger, emptiness, guilt, betrayal, self-doubt. Find a way to vent your feelings so they don't get the best of you.

2. Formulate a game plan. Develop a plan of action that will allow you to capitalize upon your new situation by identifying opportunities that are more in keeping with your skills, interests, and values.

3. Develop a strategy against your liabilities. Good lawyers always address the weaknesses in their cases. Likewise, good job hunters must develop a case that effectively offsets their weaknesses.

4. Take care of yourself. Eat properly, exercise, and get plenty of sleep. Make social events a priority. You need time to laugh and feel connected to people you care about.

43. Emotional Preparation for the Job Search

Many job hunters mistakenly jump into the thick of their job search without sufficient preparation. Unresolved feelings—more than any other single factor—do the most to undermine even the most sophisticated job-search efforts. So, let's start our job-search checklist with a little mental and emotional housecleaning.

Place a check mark next to those situations that apply to you.

☐ I am still angry at my last boss because he/she didn't

    ☐ appreciate   ☐ recognize   ☐ protect   ☐ reward me

☐ I am too old to find a new job.

☐ I do not have enough experience to find a job.

☐ My last employer will give me a good recommendation, but I know my skills are not really up to par.

☐ My résumé looks good, but I am afraid interviewers will discover that I am hiding

    ☐ employment gaps   ☐ the fact that I got fired

    ☐ my poor performance record.

☐ I have no idea what I want to do.

☐ I am not qualified for the job I want.

☐ I feel like no one will give me a chance to prove myself.

☐ I could never compete for a good job.

If one or more of these situations apply to you, you may want to consider working with a qualified therapist or career counselor, job club, or support group, in order to resolve any negative feelings that may interfere with a productive job-search outcome.

44. 7 Steps for Putting Your Psychological House in Order

Finally, the moment of truth. You know what you want; your paperwork is in place to get it; you are ready for action. The next step is to organize a well-focused job search campaign. Before you do that, however, you must develop the right attitudes toward your search. Without the proper mindset, even the most well-organized job search campaign is likely to fail.

☐ 1. Develop an active (rather than a reactive) attitude. This means that you must initiate contact with potential employers. Don't wait for them to come to you. Since most jobs are filled in the "hidden" or unadvertised job market, simply reading the Sunday newspaper want ads does not constitute a job search.

☐ 2. It's going to take some time. Although there have been many studies conducted on the subject, no one can really tell you how long it will take. Focus on the day-to-day activities rather than the end goal. Reward yourself mentally when you successfully initiate and make contact with potential resources. If a tangible job offer is your only recognized measure of success, it may be demoralizing to feel like you are looking at an endless stream of failures.

☐ 3. Job-hunting skills can and should be learned. When you do make mistakes, don't spend a lot of mental time and energy berating yourself about them. Try to focus on where you went wrong so that you will not repeat the errors of the past. Could you have interviewed better? Did you follow up with a thank-you note? Was your cover letter addressed to a specific person? Zero in on areas that need improvement, then improve them.

☐ 4. Job hunters court rejection on a daily basis. It comes with the territory of looking for new work. Try not to personalize those rejections or you will lose confidence in yourself. Confidence, of course, plays a crucial role in your success.

☐ 5. Job hunters have a tendency to isolate themselves because they are embarrassed or ashamed of their situation. This is anathema to both your mental health and a successful job search outcome. Stay involved in your normal activities; keep up a social life; communicate with family and friends. Join a support group of job hunters to help you stay motivated. Accountability can be very important.

☐ 6. Try to develop a positive attitude. Unemployment, although sometimes traumatic, also provides opportunity for growth. It helps if you can keep your situation in perspective. Remember that it is a temporary, not a permanent, situation. This, too, shall pass.

☐ 7. A long-term perspective really helps. Try to place your current situation in the context of an entire career. Use this time to grow, learn, and redirect your energies.

HINT: You are still a person even though you don't have a job. Watch your self-esteem; it is the key to future employment. Stay active in social and professional activities. It will remind you who you are.

45. Where the Jobs Are

People and printed information are the keys to job leads. A quick lesson in job market structure will illustrate this point.

Advertised Listings

1. Local newspaper and specialty publications such as the *National Business Employment Weekly* and *National Ad Search* contain help-wanted listings for a diverse industries and occupations.

2. Trade journals and newspapers provide industry or field-specific information. Example: Professionals seeking work in higher education usually turn to *The Chronicle of Higher Education* as a primary resource tool. Lawyers in Chicago usually read the *Chicago Daily Law Bulletin*. For a job in the federal government, try *Federal Career Opportunities*. Your school or business librarian can help you find the publications you need.

3. Professional associations also print newsletters with job listings. Some may also have a job bank where employers can list open positions. The *Encyclopedia of Associations* or *National Trade and Professional Associations* directories provide fairly comprehensive listings of associations in most industries.

4. Public job services also have job listings available to job hunters.

5. Human resource departments may post open positions on bulletin boards or maintain a published list of positions currently available. You usually can call or drop by in person to read the job descriptions for yourself.

6. School placement offices and individual departments often maintain bulletin boards with job listings.

Unadvertised openings

1. Executive recruiters, or "headhunters," are retained by individual client companies to fill specific openings. Often, these positions have not been advertised. The *Directory of Executive Recruiters* will help you identify recruiters who specialize in your industry or career field. Then, you can network your way in, send a résumé with cover letter, or telephone them directly.

2. Most often, unadvertised positions exist in the minds of employers. Networking, direct mail, and telemarketing strategies can put you in a position to talk to people who may be interested in hiring you. Although this is listed last on this checklist, it is the mainstay of every good job search.

Of course, you can always use published materials to access the hidden job market. Read the answers to the hidden job market quiz in the next section to discover the key.

46. Test Your Hidden Job Market IQ

Experts estimate that 85 percent of all new positions are filled through the "hidden" or "underground" job market. The following quiz will test your knowledge of the hidden job market. Examine each of the following 10 methods for discovering the hidden job market. Is it an effective method? Answer True or False.

		True	False
1.	Networking	☐	☐
2.	Informational Interviews	☐	☐
3.	Help Wanted Ads	☐	☐
4.	Direct Mail Campaigns	☐	☐
5.	Executive Recruiters	☐	☐
6.	Employment Agencies	☐	☐
7.	Telemarketing	☐	☐
8.	Temporary Help Agencies	☐	☐
9.	College Placement Offices	☐	☐
10.	Trade Journals	☐	☐

Answer Key

1. True. Employment experts agree that networking is the best way to uncover job leads in the underground job market. Based on the concept of the "old boys network," this relies upon your ability to establish contacts who can give you inside information on job leads. Use relatives, neighbors, friends, colleagues, clients and (ex)employers to create your own individualized networks. Expand your network through professional associations, clubs, and other membership groups.

2. True. Informational interviews—in which you interview for information about companies and industries rather than specific jobs—are also an excellent way to uncover leads. If you are able to establish good rapport with the interviewers, they will inevitably tell you about specific job openings in their organizations.

3. True. The help wanted ads normally are considered the advertised or publicized job market, rather than the hidden market. However, a savvy job hunter can use the ads creatively to identify companies that may be hiring. That information can be used to initiate discussions about other job possibilities.

4. True. Writing letters to the hiring authorities in companies that interest you, regardless of whether a specific position has been advertised, is a good way to locate unadvertised positions.

5. True. Typically, executive recruiters (also called "headhunters") work for client companies rather than individual candidates. However, most recruiters will do some selective candidate marketeering. Use networking strategies to establish relationships with recruiters who may be in a position to hire you.

6. True. Employment agencies do work from specific listings; however, they also have relationships with various employer companies. If a candidate's credentials are particularly appealing, an employment agency recruiter may be willing to do some prospecting for you.

7. True. The telephone is one of the best ways to uncover job leads. Use the Yellow Pages listings or directories from professional associations to create a target list of companies and individuals.

8. True. Temporary or interim jobs are an excellent way to gain a foothold into a company. From the inside, you can initiate discussions with hiring authorities to learn more about their needs, while establishing your own credibility at the same time.

9. True. Many colleges provide alumni counseling services which includes individual counseling, newsletters with job listings, and alumni directories. A membership directory can be an invaluable resource tool to identify potential networking contacts.

10. True. Trade journals are an excellent source of job-hunting information. Use stories to glean inside information about organizational developments that will allow you to identify key players and develop an educated job-search strategy.

47. The Myth of Networking

Networking has been identified by many employment experts as the number one way to find new work. Some cynical folks believe this is just a fancy new word for an old idea: namely, that it's not *what* you know, but *who* you know, that really counts.

Yes and no. The concept of networking is based on the "old boys network" of years past, in which it was common for information about new jobs to travel by word of mouth. For example, if Joe was looking for a new sales manager, he might tell his friend, Bob. If Bob knew that his friend Ken was looking for a new job, he might tell Ken to call Joe. On the other hand, Ken might not be in the market for a new job right now, but he can easily pass the information along to his former colleague Jeff. And so on and so forth.

Things have not changed all that much. Savvy job hunters realize that they must have access to the hiring grapevine. This means casting their networking net as widely and deeply as possible so that people will know and remember them when new jobs do appear.

While it does matter who you know right this instant, it is also a question of who you can meet. Even if the people in your immediate network do not work or have jobs available in your particular industry, they may be able to recommend and refer you to others who can help. The key is to identify who you know and what you are looking for, then successfully communicate that information to your contacts. The best contacts in the world will be hard-pressed to help you if they don't know what you need.

Finally, it is a mistake to believe that it doesn't matter *what* you know. The better your skills and reputation, the greater the likelihood that people will feel motivated to pass your name along to others. Job hunters should make it their business to protect themselves on two fronts: first, by developing a solid portfolio of skills; and second, by initiating discussions with as many people as possible.

48. 7 Ways to Identify Networking Contacts

☐ 1. Determine the kind of information that you need.

☐ 2. Make a list of all your friends, acquaintances, neighbors, relatives, colleagues, and past employers. Ask these individuals if they can introduce you to someone who works in the fields, industries, or companies you would like to explore.

☐ 3. Use the *Encyclopedia of Associations* to identify any professional associations in your target area. Find out if the association has a local chapter with monthly meetings, then plan to attend.

☐ 4. Determine whether the professional associations have membership directories. Use this directory to identify individuals who work in the areas that interest you. Call or write to introduce yourself, discuss your qualifications, and ask for information or possible job leads.

☐ 5. Join activities. Clubs, hobbies, sports, and other extracurricular activities can provide an ideal informal setting to meet new people and develop new referral sources.

☐ 6. Follow through on every appropriate lead.

☐ 7. Remember that "new" isn't always "better." Stay in touch with the people you already know. Keep them apprised of your progress. And always say thank-you to them for their guidance and support.

Networking tip: Membership directories can be a veritable bonanza of networking information. One job hunter ran her entire job search out of the membership directory of her professional communications group. She called up each person in the directory, identified herself, briefly stated her qualifications and job objective, and asked for possible leads. She was so successful that she turned up six unlisted positions in the very first week.

Another job hunter ran his entire job search out of his college alumni directory. He also called up the members who were listed, identified himself, stated his qualifications and job objective, and asked for possible leads. He, too, turned up many unlisted positions.

To use this strategy successfully yourself, prepare your own telephone script outlining the points which were just mentioned. Practice your script on family and friends. Solicit their feedback, perfect your technique, then start making calls.

Sample Telephone Script

Hello. My name is Jerry Smith. I received your name from the membership directory of the American Society for Training and Development. I was wondering if you have a few minutes to talk with me?

I have been working as a corporate trainer for the last five years, where I was involved in designing and delivering training programs for insurance companies. I have decided to look for a new position outside the insurance industry. When I saw your name in the directory, it occurred to me that you might be able to provide me with some information about training positions in your field.

Do you know of any other positions that might be available or anyone who might be hiring? If so, I would appreciate the opportunity to speak with them directly. In the meantime, I would like to send you a copy of my résumé. If you do hear of any specific openings, I would appreciate it if you would let me know.

Thank you for your time. I enjoyed talking to you.

49. Sources of Networking Contacts

At my current employer:

_____

_____

_____

_____

_____

From former employers:

_____

_____

_____

_____

At school:

_____

_____

_____

_____

From professional activities:

_____

_____

_____

_____

Through family and friends:

_____

_____

_____

_____

From neighbors and community acquaintances:

_____

_____

_____

_____

Through customers and clients:

_____

_____

_____

_____

At clubs and social organizations:

_____

_____

_____

_____

From service people (attorneys, bankers, doctors, hairdressers, waitresses, mail carrier):

_____

_____

_____

_____

Through other job hunters:

_____

_____

_____

_____

Other:

_____

_____

_____

_____

_____

_____

_____

50. Networking Worksheets

Worksheet #1

Type of information needed: _____

_____

_____

Name of contact: _____

Position (if applicable): _____

Employer (if applicable): _____

Address: _____

_____

_____

Telephone: (work) _____

(home) _____

Referral source: _____

Date contacted: _____

Method of contact: _____
    (telephone or letter)

Results of discussion: _____

_____

_____

_____

_____

Follow-up (yes or no): _____

Date of follow-up: _____

Method of follow-up: _____

Results: _____

_____

_____

_____

_____

Notes: _____

_____

_____

_____

_____

Worksheet #2

Type of information needed: _____

_____

_____

Name of contact: _____

Position (if applicable): _____

Employer (if applicable): _____

Address: _____

_____

_____

Telephone: (work) _____

(home) _____

Referral source: _____

Date contacted: _____

Method of contact: _____

Results of discussion: _____

_____

_____

_____

_____

Follow-up: _____

Date of follow-up: _____

Method of follow-up _____

Results: _____

_____

_____

_____

_____

Notes: _____

_____

_____

_____

_____

HINT: Seventy-five percent of all new positions are obtained by developing personal contacts. Make a concerted effort to expand your contact base by joining professional groups, social activities, and other group activities.

HINT: Out of sight means out of mind in job-hunting land. Stay in touch with your networking contacts by keeping them apprised of your efforts. If one of their suggestions or job leads proved particularly helpful, let them know. This will motivate them to continue thinking about—and helping—you.

51. 4 More Job-Hunting Myths

Myth #1. A headhunter will find me a job.
False. Headhunters work for client companies, not individual job hunters. Although recruiters may do some selective candidate marketeering, they should never be relied upon as a primary job-search method.

Myth #2. The help-wanted ads are the best way to find a new job.
False. Most new positions are filled through the hidden, rather than the advertised, job market. Every job-search strategy should include at least two ways to access leads from this underground reservoir.

Myth #3. Letters and applications should always go through the personnel department.
False. Personnel or human resources departments are often in the business of screening out candidates. Since they receive so many applications, it may be difficult for you to get the personal attention you need from personnel offices. Many employment experts suggest that you initiate contact directly with the person who manages the department or division where you are interested in working. Often, these people are in a position to take a personal interest in your candidacy—and have even been known to create brand new positions for interesting candidates.

Myth #4. More is better.
False. A qualitative, individualized job search usually works significantly better than the broadcast approach. Selectively identify the organizations you want to contact, then write an individualized letter to a specific interviewer reflecting your interest in that particular company. Nothing turns off hiring authorities quicker than a job hunter who says, "Dear Employer: I need a job, any job. So hire me." Employers want to know why you want to work for *them*, and why you are qualified to do so. If you don't know the answer to those questions, back up and do some research first.

52. An 8-Point Checklist for Using Want Ads

Sooner or later, almost every job hunter turns to the want ads for help. Knowing how and when to use advertised listings is an important part of every job search.

☐ 1. Identify the newspapers, magazines, and trade journals that match your qualifications.

☐ 2. Read the *entire* classified section from two or three past issues to get a feeling for how the information is organized.

☐ 3. Make a list of those section headings (such as administrative, health care, education, personnel, and others) that are more relevant to you. Be sure you check those headings each and every time you read the ads.

☐ 4. Cut out or make copies of ads that require a response.

☐ 5. Review the ad carefully before responding in order to prepare your response. How are you expected to respond—by telephone or letter? For telephone responses, prepare your script in advance. What qualifications are required? Why do you feel you are qualified for the position? On the other hand, if the ad says, "No phone calls, please"—*don't* call! You will only alienate a potential employer.

☐ 6. When a résumé is required, always include a cover letter describing your interest in and qualifications for the position. Stick as closely to the terms of the ad as possible. Highlight those pieces of your experience that are most relevant. If you need more information, call the employer first and ask to know more about the position. The more you know, the better off you will be.

☐ 7. Make sure that you include a telephone number where you can be reached. Otherwise, you are wasting your time and effort sending out résumés.

☐ 8. Wait approximately one week, then follow up your letter and résumé with a telephone call. In that conversation, confirm that your résumé has been received, ask about the hiring process, discuss your qualifications, and request an interview. Some employment experts estimate that follow-up telephone calls increase the number of interviews received by 25 percent or more.

53. A Quick Guide to 7 Kinds of Employment Services

There are many different types of employment experts who can help you with your career and job-search needs. It is important to know exactly what each individual or organization can provide in order to select the most appropriate services for your needs.

1. Career counselors are retained by individuals who require career/life planning and development and/or job-search assistance. They may work in private practice, educational institutions, or social service agencies. Services may include individual consultations, vocational testing, support groups, job skills workshops, and assistance with résumé preparation. Most counselors may charge on an hourly or a flat-fee basis. Nonprofit organizations may offer sliding scale or low-cost services to various populations. (**Note:** Advance-fee career marketing firms have come under close scrutiny by the Better Business Bureau for their controversial practice of charging substantial upfront fees ranging from $1,500 to $6,000. Before you sign on with one of these firms, make sure you know exactly what you are getting for your money.)

2. Employment or placement counselors work for employment agencies. They serve as intermediaries between client companies and individuals who are looking for work. When working with employment counselors, it is important to be clear about the type of work/job you are seeking. Also, make sure that *all fees are paid by the client company*. No job hunter should ever pay a placement fee to an employment agency.

3. Executive recruiters ("headhunters") are retained by client companies to fill executive-level or professional positions. They may be hired by a company on a retainer or contingency basis to fill specific openings. Their fees are always paid by the client company. Since recruiters are usually rich in contacts, they are good people to have on your side. Try to identify those recruiters who specialize in your field or industry; then, if you can, network your way into their good graces.

4. Human resources/personnel representatives are individuals who are employed by specific companies to recruit, screen, and fill specific job openings.

5. Outplacement counselors provide individual job counseling, testing, workshops, and résumé assistance to individuals who have lost their jobs. Their fees are paid by the employer/company. Occasionally, outplacement counselors serve individual walk-in clients, but this is seldom their primary business.

6. Résumé services organize, write, and type résumés for individual job hunters.

7. Testing services provide aptitude, interest, and personality tests for individuals with career choice and planning needs. Not all testing services are comprehensive.

54. 11 Things
Career Counselors Do

The role of a career counselor has often been likened to that of a career "coach." Although counselors vary in training, philosophy, and services, they usually provide one or more of the following services:

1. Provide individual evaluations and counseling to establish, clarify, and develop career/life goals.

2. Conduct job support groups and career workshops.

3. Administer and interpret tests to evaluate abilities, interests, values, personality, and organizational style.

4. Assign activities and exercises to develop self-knowledge and increase job market awareness.

5. Teach job-hunting strategies and skills.

6. Assist with résumé preparation.

7. Use counseling techniques to improve career decision-making skills.

8. Provide support during stressful transitions.

9. Help resolve emotional and interpersonal conflicts.

10. Aid clients in developing career plans.

11. Coordinate services with other helping professionals.

55. Do You Need Professional Career Counseling?

If any of the situations listed below characterize your work life, you may be a good candidate for career counseling:

☐ I always get stuck in dead-end jobs.

☐ I don't know what I want to be when I "grow up."

☐ I am bored with my work.

☐ I usually get fired for "personality conflicts."

☐ I never like my coworkers.

☐ My interests are too general and need to be focused.

☐ My interests are narrowly defined, and my field offers little or no room for career advancement.

☐ I have reached the top of my pay scale and career ladder.

☐ I have more abilities than my job can utilize.

☐ My work feels meaningless.

☐ My career expectations have never been realized.

☐ I change jobs a lot.

☐ I have trouble setting and meeting goals.

56. The "Headhunter" Connection

Executive recruiters, also known as "headhunters," can provide valuable job-search assistance. Follow these guidelines to make the best use of this job-search resource.

1. Recruiters work for client companies rather than individuals. Therefore, you should not expect them to have a responsibility to market your credentials. However, they do have bona fide job listings to fill. They are also rich in contacts, so it makes sense to make friends with a recruiter.

2. Networking is usually the best way to make a connection. Ask your friends and colleagues to recommend you to recruiters they have worked with in the past. Also, if you have recruiter connections from your own past employment, don't be shy about using them. A good recruiter knows that clients and candidates are interchangeable. Someone who is employed today may be unemployed tomorrow, and vice versa.

3. Make a trip to the library for the *Directory of Executive Recruiters*. Use this directory to determine the names of recruiters who specialize in your industry or job functions. Selectively contact those individuals first. Don't blanket the recruiter marketplace with unsolicited résumés.

4. Some recruiters suggest that candidates use the telephone first to establish rapport with a recruiter, then follow up with a résumé and personal interview. Others like it the other way around. You may want to try it both ways and see what works best for you.

5. Follow up résumés with telephone calls. If possible, set up an interview.

6. Don't show up on a recruiter's doorstep "hat in hand." Try to offer something in the way of information or client leads. Since recruiting is the ultimate networking profession, you may have more to offer than you realize.

7. Don't get mad at recruiters because they don't send you out on enough interviews. Remember, they work for client companies, not for candidates. A recruiter doesn't owe you a job.

57. 5 Rules for Connecting With Recruiters

Steve Xagas, president of the recruiting firm Xagas & Associates, recommends that job hunters follow these five rules for contacting and working with recruiters.

1. Use the *Directory of Executive Recruiters* to identify recruiters who specialize in your field or industry. Another source of information is John Sibbald's new book, *The Career-Makers: America's Top 100 Executive Recruiters*, which also includes a list of the leading recruiters' specialties. Once you have found recruiters in your field, send them a résumé and cover letter describing your interest and qualifications.

2. Network your way into a recruiter's heart. Talk to friends and colleagues who have worked with a recruiter they like and respect.
   "A recommendation from an existing client is one of the best ways to get a recruiter's ear," Xagas says. "We listen when our clients speak."

3. Offer the recruiters something in return for their time and attention. Pass along some information, a referral to a potential client company, or the name of another job hunter who may be a good candidate for a different type of position.
   "Too many job hunters act and feel like they have nothing to offer," Xagas says. "Recruiting is the ultimate networking profession. We are always on the lookout for people and information. Job hunters who can offer that have something we want."

4. Don't expect a recruiter to get you a job. Recruiters work for client companies, not individuals. However, if you are able to establish a good relationship with recruiters, they may be willing to keep their eyes and ears open for you.
   Steve Xagas recommends working with recruiters who work on retainer rather than on assignment. "Recruiters who work on retainer are contact-rich," he says. "They have the ear of people within an organization who are in a position to create new positions for the right candidate."

5. Approach recruiters selectively. Never work with more than two or three at one time. Otherwise, you may dilute your efforts and lose credibility with a recruiter. However, if a recruiter is not being useful to you, don't waste your time. Move on to someone else who may be of more help.

58. Recruiter Connection Worksheet

Name of recruiter: _____

Address: _____

_____

Telephone: _____

Area of specialization: _____

Date of contact: _____

Method of contact: _____

Referral source: _____

Results: _____

_____

_____

_____

_____

_____

Follow-up: _____

_____

_____

_____

Name of recruiter: _____

Address: _____

_____

Telephone: _____

Area of specialization: _____

Date of contact: _____

Method of contact: _____

Referral source: _____

Results: _____

_____

_____

_____

_____

Follow-up: _____

_____

_____

_____

59. Shopping for an Employment Agency

Finding an employment agency that can really be of service to you in your job search requires a little shopping savvy. You may want to ask the following questions and keep a record of their responses.

1. Do they specialize in any one industry or area?

2. What kinds of individuals do they prefer to serve/place?

3. Who pays the fee?

4. Do you have to work with them exclusively?

5. Do they provide assistance with résumés?

6. Will they coach you for interviews?

7. Do they have job orders that match your background and skills?

Employment Agency Log

Name of agency: _____

Area of specialization: _____

Who pays fee: _____

Services: _____

Name of agency: _____

Area of specialization: _____

Who pays fee: _____

Services: _____

60. 9 Tips About Job Fairs

Job fairs are a wonderful place to gather information about potential employers and conduct informational interviews. Watch your local newspapers for listings of upcoming events, then gear yourself up for an interesting day's work.

1. Allow yourself plenty of time. Most job fairs are at least one or two full days. Plan to spend the better part of one day at the event.

2. Many job fairs have individual workshops. Determine whether any of these talks are relevant to your interests. When you set up your event schedule, be sure you leave time for the workshops that interest you.

3. Dress for success. Many employers will conduct initial screening interviews. It is extremely important that you make a good first impression. When in doubt about attire, always err on the side of conservatism— subdued suits with white shirts are usually safe for both sexes. No gym shoes, please.

4. Bring plenty of copies of your résumé to circulate. Also, check to see if the conference planners circulate résumés in advance. If so, submit yours early and often.

5. Scout out the room before you begin so that you can plan your time effectively. Determine which employers you want most to meet. Make yourself a priority list. Also, create a backup log of "maybes" in case you have some time left over at the end.

6. Prepare and rehearse a three-minute speech describing who you are, what kind of work you are looking for, and what your qualifications are to do the work. If possible, read through the company's printed materials and talk to the recruiter informally before you arrange for a more personal interview.

7. Give yourself some breathing space. Most job fair interviews last anywhere from 5 to 15 minutes. After each interview, take a few minutes to reflect on what you learned and how you performed. Jot down the recruiter's name and a few notes about your conversation to jog your memory later on. Then move on to the next interview.

8.   Be sure to collect any handouts or printed materials furnished by companies on your priority or "maybe" lists where you suspect you may not have enough time left to interview. You may want to follow up later on.

9.   When you get back to your office or home, organize the information you received. If there is any follow-up work necessary—in the form of thank-you letters, reference letters, or other materials to be sent—be sure to follow through on your discussion. Elaborate upon any information you may need or want later. It's easier to recall that information now while it's still in your short-term memory.

61. 12 Keys to Long-Distance Job Hunting

Long-distance job hunting has some built-in obstacles. It may be difficult to identify leads, make contacts, and conduct interviews. Employers have a tendency to hire familiar faces. Although you know you are not a visitor from outer space—just another city—you may be perceived like you are an alien from another planet. To overcome these resistances, familiarize yourself with the city's resources as much as possible. Practice your telephone skills—you are going to need them.

1. If you have any contacts at all in your target location, start by enlisting them as allies. Ask them to send you a copy of the local telephone Yellow Pages. Also, you will need the name of any major newspapers, business directories, or job-hunting books. Of course, people contacts are also welcome.

2. If you have no contacts in the area, you can track down this information yourself. Call the chamber of commerce in your target city to obtain any business directories or information that may be available.

3. If you currently live in a major city, your local business librarian may also be able to help you locate telephone books, business directories, and newspapers. Even if the library doesn't have the actual publications, the librarian can give you the names you are looking for so that you can obtain the materials yourself.

4. Plan to subscribe to the local newspapers for a while. In addition to the Sunday paper with classified listings, you will learn more about the events and happenings in that city. This will help you wear the "insider's hat" you need to get hired.

5. If you belong to a professional association with a national membership, ask for the names of people who head up the chapters in your target areas. Network with those people by telephone to make new contacts and learn more about the city's resources.

6. If you do not belong to a professional association, use the *Encyclopedia of Associations* to determine which groups have national memberships with local chapters. Join at least one group that has local chapters in *both* cities.

7. Use the membership directory to network. Conduct informational interviews by telephone. If your budget is limited, you may want to make initial contact by letter, but you will need to talk to your contacts by phone at some time.

8. Network with the people you know for any contacts they may have in your target areas. Don't worry about whether the new people actually work in your field. They may be able to introduce you to others who do.

9. Once you have the names of potential contacts, write a letter introducing yourself. Or better yet, call them up to talk. Discuss your interest in relocating. Ask for job search advice about how you can best establish yourself as a serious candidate from afar. Request names of people and places they might recommend.

10. Ditto for executive recruiters or headhunters. Use the *Directory of Executive Recruiters* to obtain names of recruiters who operate in your target city and industry. You can then telephone or write. Of course, if you can find a way to network your way in, that will work even better.

11. Plan an in-city visit, preferably around an industry conference, trade show, or meeting, so that you can make as many contacts as possible. Schedule your time carefully. Reconnect with networking contacts. Make plans to meet them—even if you know they currently don't have any specific job openings. The more familiar your face, the better your chances will be.

12. Stay in touch with your contacts. When you are far away, it is a little too easy to forget you. Don't let that happen.

HINT: The more familiar and comfortable you feel with your target city, the greater likelihood that you will succeed in your job search. Take time (even from afar) to learn as much as possible about your future home.

62. Managing Your Finances During a Job Search

Unemployment is never fun. It usually means tightening your belt a little to make ends meet. This worksheet should help organize your financial thinking.

1. Are you eligible for unemployment compensation? Figure the amount here.

   _____

2. Severance pay is often part of a termination package. This may be anywhere from one week's pay to one full year. Have you discussed this with your employer? If so, how much are you entitled to?

   _____

3. Are you vested in pension or profit-sharing plans? Figure the amount here.

   _____

4. What about insurance benefits? Some employers will agree to maintain you on their health insurance plan for a period of time beyond your employment. Check this out.

5. What about outplacement counseling to help you find new work? This benefit can save you many months of time and effort.

6. List any other sources of income.

   Monthly family income: _____

   Property rentals: _____

   Interest/dividends: _____

   Part-time work: _____

   Other: _____

7. You may want to supplement your income through part-time or temporary jobs. List any skills you may have that are marketable for this type of work.

_____

_____

8. Check the telephone book for names of temporary agencies that may serve you.

_____

_____

9. List any contacts that may be able to provide you with interim work.

_____

_____

10. Estimate your income from temporary work.

_____

_____

11. Now calculate your expenses. Try to determine places where you can cut back.

Rent/mortgage: _____

Utilities: _____

Telephone: _____

Automobile expenses: _____

Insurance: _____

Loans: _____

Clothing: _____

Food: _____

Household expenses: _____

Entertainment: _____

Miscellaneous: _____

Total: _____

12. Subtract your expenses from your income. How long can you realistically afford unemployment?

_____

_____

13. Should it take longer to find employment, can you think of other ways to earn extra money? List them here.

_____

_____

_____

_____

_____

_____

_____

_____

63. 5 Time Management Tips for Job Hunters

Finding the time to conduct a successful job search is often a problem, particularly for employed job hunters. To get better control of your time, try following these guidelines.

1. Block out periods of time for various job search activities. Early morning hours, lunch hours, vacation time, sick days, evenings, and weekends all can be pressed into service for a job search.

2. For streamlined efficiency, organize your job search activities into categories, such as making telephone calls, sending out résumés, and setting up interviews. Set goals to accomplish activities in each category.

3. Reward yourself when you have completed a task by doing something you really enjoy.

4. Zero in on your tendencies to procrastinate. Don't let yourself be sidetracked by things that are really less important. If you do, you will never reach your end goal.

5. Find the optimal place to work. If there are too many distractions at home, go to the library. If you don't have enough privacy at the office, find another place to make calls. View each obstacle as an opportunity to practice problem-solving skills.

Job-Search Log

Activity: _____

Time spent: _____

Results: _____

_____

Activity: _____

Time spent: _____

Results: _____

_____

Activity: _____

Time spent: _____

Results: _____

_____

Activity: _____

Time spent: _____

Results: _____

_____

Activity: _____

Time spent: _____

Results: _____

_____

Activity: _____

Time spent: _____

Results: _____

_____

Activity: _____

Time spent: _____

Results: _____

_____

64. 9-Point
Job Search Checklist

	Yes	No
1. Do you check the newspapers and specialty publications on a regular basis?	☐	☐
2. Do you subscribe to at least one (and preferably two or three) trade journal with classified listings?	☐	☐
3. Are you a member of at least one (and preferably two or three) professional association in your industry?	☐	☐
4. Do you have a copy of the membership directory for your school or professional association to use for networking purposes?	☐	☐
5. Have you submitted your name to the association job bank, if they have one?	☐	☐
6. Have you talked to your alumni placement offices about services they might offer?	☐	☐
7. Do you check their bulletin board and newsletters for job listings?	☐	☐
8. Have you established a networking strategy—methods and places where you can connect with people who can help you?	☐	☐
9. Are you using directories and other printed materials to identify companies or organizations that might be in a position to hire you?	☐	☐

HINT: Rejection is an inevitable part of every job search. When you do receive that fateful "Thanks, but no thanks" letter, try not to take it too personally. Instead, thank the employer for considering you, reiterate your interest in working for the company or organization, and express an interest in future openings. Check back periodically to determine whether any new positions are available.

HINT: Never confuse silence with rejection. Follow up your letters and résumés with telephone calls. Make sure that your correspondence was received *and* read. Use that follow-up call as an opportunity to convince potential employers that you really do deserve an interview. You'll be surprised by the results. Many employers admire assertiveness.

HINT: Reward yourself for successful job-search activities. Every time a new networking contact is established, a job lead pans out, or an interview is successfully negotiated, a piece of your job-search mission has been accomplished. Recognize and applaud your efforts. If you focus too prematurely (and much) on the job offer as the only tangible sign of success, you will become too easily discouraged. The "one day at a time" mentality definitely applies to a successful job hunting strategy.

65. 15 Keys to Job-Search Success

1. You have determined your job-search objective.

2. You know (and can communicate) why you are qualified for this work.

3. You have a good résumé targeted toward this objective.

4. You know how to identify job leads.

5. You have a networking strategy.

6. You know how to communicate what you are looking for.

7. You are not afraid to ask for help.

8. You have job-search goals.

9. You have organized a job-search strategy.

10. You feel positive about your job search.

11. You know how to ask for help.

12. You have (or can create) a support system.

13. You know it's going to take some time.

14. You are willing to work hard at finding new work.

15. You are prepared to be patient and flexible.

> **HINT:** Despite your best efforts, there may be a time when your job search stalls. Perhaps you have exhausted your networking contacts, your job leads have dried up, or you have just missed out on several job offers. You can weather the storm by developing a long-term perspective. This lull is *usually* temporary. Focus on how you can revitalize your search. Recontact former contacts, join new professional groups, and practice new interviewing styles and approaches. Sooner or later, your ship is bound to come in. If not, seek professional career counseling—you may be doing something wrong.

4

Successful Interviews

"What corrupts communication?
Anger, fear, prejudice, egotism, and
envy."

—Guy de Maupassant

"Look to your speech, lest it mar your
fortune."

—William Shakespeare

66. 15 Commonly Asked Interview Questions

The self-assessment and job market exploration activities lay the groundwork for successful interviews. Your task is to communicate to employers how and why you would fit well into their organization. The more you are able to determine how your skills, interests, values, and personality fit into their scheme of things, the greater likelihood that you will succeed. Of course, you can't just know that information—you also have to communicate it. Try preparing, and then rehearsing, your responses to these 15 commonly asked interview questions.

1. What can you tell me about yourself? (Emphasize those aspects of yourself that are particularly relevant for this job.)

_____

_____

_____

_____

_____

2. Why did you leave your last position? (Concentrate on your desire for new challenges rather than admitting you left because you couldn't stand your boss.)

_____

_____

_____

_____

_____

3. What are your strengths?

_____

_____

_____

_____

4. What are your weaknesses? (For this question, try to frame strengths as if they are weaknesses—"I tend to work too hard;" "I try to be too much of a perfectionist"—instead of volunteering that your work is sloppy or you show up late.)

_____

_____

_____

_____

5. What were your major accomplishments in each of your jobs? (Refer to your résumé worksheet, if necessary.)

_____

_____

_____

_____

6. Why are there gaps in your work history? (Frame the truth here, in the best possible light, but make sure employers understand that this is not a red flag with regard to your capabilities—"I needed some time to re-evaluate my career direction and priorities;" "I wanted to look around carefully before taking a new job in order to find the best possible match."

_____

_____

_____

_____

7. Why should I hire you? (Reflect on your skills and accomplishments; match them up with your understanding of the position responsibilities as well as company goals and values—"I am a highly motivated self-starter who has always taken the initiative to develop new ideas and programs. For example, (elaborate). You have described yourself as a very aggressive person who really wants to take the market by storm. Given my history of accomplishments and working style, I think we would make an excellent team.")

_____

_____

_____

_____

8. What was your relationship with your boss like? (If it wasn't the greatest, be honest but tactful—"I respected her, but I don't believe she took advantage of my full potential.")

_____

_____

_____

_____

9. How do you usually get along with your coworkers? (Try to portray yourself as a team player, if possible.)

_____

_____

_____

10. Describe your work personality. (Be positive, of course. Refer back to your personality profile to refresh your memory.)

_____

_____

_____

11. Which job did you like the least? Why? (Don't dwell on money here; few jobs pay as well as we'd like. Instead, try to pick an experience that will show in a roundabout way what you *do* want—"I liked my job at XYZ Corp. the least because I was unable to utilize my broad range of abilities, and there seemed to be no room for advancement.")

_____

_____

_____

12. Which job did you like the most? Why?

_____

_____

_____

13. If you could do things differently, what would you change? (Emphasize something you did well and discuss how it could have been even better.)

_____

_____

_____

14. Have you ever been fired? Why? (Remember, frame your answer as positively as possible. Don't try to whitewash the truth; employers will see through this. If you made mistakes, take responsibility for them, but demonstrate that you learned something from these mistakes, so that you will not repeat them—"I had an argument with my boss and he fired me for insubordination. I realize, in retrospect, that I must be less impulsive and show more respect for authority. I can assure you that this is no longer a problem."

_____

_____

_____

_____

15. What do you want to be doing five years from now? (Make sure your answer reflects some career growth—"I hope to be an assistant manager by then"—and desire to remain in the company. Employers don't want people who will stagnate or decide to leave after a year.)

_____

_____

_____

_____

HINT: Interviews are a little bit like blind dates. Both parties are trying to find common interests and language, in order to evaluate whether they want to see each other again. Although some people "fall in love" on the first date, it often takes more time. Similarly, first interviews are screening interviews in which you are trying to learn enough about each other to make the "second date" decision. You can break the ice with small talk. Take some time to share a personal experience, comment on the interviewer's office, even discuss the weather. This will ease the way for the more serious discussions that follow.

HINT: Resolve any negative feelings you have for your former employer outside the interview. Interviewees who complain about past bosses or situations only shed doubt upon their own credibility. As the saying goes, "You can catch more flies with honey than with vinegar." Demonstrate through your actions and language that you will be a nice person to have on the team.

67. 22 Interview Do's and Don'ts

1. Do dress properly. The best rule of thumb: dress conservatively and professionally. Try to anticipate how the interviewer will be dressed, and mirror that behavior.

2. Don't look grim. Although you may be nervous and tense, a smile can be a great ice-breaker. Remember, interviewers are people, too. They usually respond to warmth.

3. Do listen attentively. Show honest interest and enthusiasm. The interview is no place for cool objectivity. Employers want people to care.

4. Don't sit passively by and expect the interviewer to control the interview. Actively ask questions, assert your ideas, and express your thoughts. *Communicate!*

5. Do research on the organization and, if possible, the interviewer ahead of time. This expresses interest and enables you to have a more educated and interesting conversation.

6. Don't be late. Leave plenty of time to get to the interview. Make sure you have proper directions. First impressions are crucial.

7. Do prepare some "canned" answers to common interview questions in advance. This will help you be comfortable with the information you plan to present.

8. Don't deliver answers to your interview questions like you are making a speech. You may have rehearsed these answers, but you don't want them to sound that way. Make conversation, not presentations.

9. Do ask intelligent questions. Inquire about job responsibilities, company goals, and other related topics. Be prepared to demonstrate how and why you are the best candidate for the job.

10. Don't initiate money or benefits conversations until you have a job offer. Once you have an actual job offer, you have a lot more negotiating power.

11. Do take extra copies of your résumé to the interview. Also, bring any additional information you might need about references, addresses, telephone numbers, and other details that may not be included on your résumé.

12. Don't call the interviewer by his or her first name, unless you are given permission.

13. Do remember the interviewer's name and use it periodically throughout the interview.

14. Don't dominate the conversation. Your answers should be succinct and direct.

15. Do answer the questions fully. One-or two-word responses usually are not effective.

16. Don't badmouth past employers, regardless of your experience. Find positive ways to couch your explanation of your circumstances.

17. Do present a confident self-image. Try not to give the impression that you are lying or have "skeletons in the closet" that may surface later.

18. Don't lie. Frame negative situations as positively as possible. Of course, you are under no obligation to tell everything. An interview is no time for "true confessions."

19. Do the best you can. Afterward, review your responses to determine which answers might have been handled differently or better. Incorporate this knowledge into your head, so that you can use it during the next interview.

20. Don't beat yourself up for making mistakes. It's part of life. The important thing is that you learn from those errors so you won't repeat them.

21. Do follow up. If you agreed to provide the interviewer with more information, make sure you do it.

22. Don't forget to send a thank-you note. In your letter, reassert your interest and qualifications.

68. 11 Things Employers Want

Basically, employers want to feel confident that you have what it takes to do the job. Qualifications usually fall into three broad categories: technical skills, general abilities, and personality characteristics. Here are some of the usual qualifications that employers look for from candidates. Do you have these qualities?

		Yes	No
1.	Objective. Do your career goals match up with the things this job and company can offer you?	☐	☐
2.	Compatibility. Will you fit into the organizational culture? Are your goals, values, and style compatible with what the organization needs and can use?	☐	☐
3.	Intelligence. Do you have enough smarts to do the job?	☐	☐
4.	Motivation. Are you motivated to work hard?	☐	☐
5.	Enthusiasm. Are you eager to do this job?	☐	☐
6.	Assertiveness. Do you have the guts to assert yourself when the situation requires? Can you stand up for your ideas and beliefs?	☐	☐
7.	Adaptability. Can you "roll with the punches"— when necessary, adapt to change?	☐	☐
8.	Maturity. Do you have good judgment? Do you know how to accept responsibility, evaluate situations, and get along with other people?	☐	☐
9.	Communication. Can you organize and articulate your thoughts effectively? Are you also a good listener who can respond to others' comments, thoughts, and needs?	☐	☐

10. Commitment. Are you serious about the work? ☐ ☐

11. Follow-through. Are you a results-oriented person? Do you set goals and follow through on your projects and goals? ☐ ☐

If you can answer "yes" to all these questions, you should have employers beating down your door! Questions to which you answered "no" point out areas you need to work on.

69. 5 Tips for Becoming a Better Listener

During interviews, communication should always be a two-way process. In order to respond effectively to interviewers, you must be able to hear and understand what they are saying. The following tips will help you become a better listener.

1. Focus your attention on what the interviewer is saying. If your mind starts to wander, consciously force yourself to listen to the *content*, even if the interviewer's vocal intonation is boring or the questions are phrased in a rambling fashion.

2. Respond with nonverbal cues. Smile or nod your head, when appropriate. This will demonstrate your interest and make the interviewer more relaxed and encouraged.

3. Resist the impulse to interrupt.

4. Listen objectively. Do not judge or criticize what you hear; doing so will only prevent you from comprehending what is being said to you.

5. Remember your purpose. Do not let yourself be distracted by things that don't really matter, like the interviewer's appearance, accent, lisp, or lipsmacking. Respond to *what* is being said rather than *how* it is being presented.

70. Handling 6 Illegal Interview Questions

Employers sometimes ask illegal questions. Obviously, this creates a sensitive problem. You can get mad and declare your right not to answer. Of course, that will probably also spoil any chance you had for a job offer. Instead, take the opportunity to play "junior psychologist." When an employer asks an illegal question, it usually reflects some reservation about your candidacy. Try to understand the *unspoken* question and respond to it. Seven examples of illegal questions—and appropriate responses—follow.

1. Q: How old are you?

    A: (For older job hunters) Your question about my age seems to reflect some concern that is not entirely clear to me. Are you concerned that I will not stay very long? If so, I can assure you that I am not a job-hopper who moves from one job to another every six months. Perhaps you are concerned about my stamina? I can assure you that I am in excellent physical health. I would be happy to have my physician attest to that fact, if necessary. Perhaps you are concerned that I will not fit in with my younger colleagues? Rest assured, this is not a problem. While working at ABC Company, many of my teammates were younger than me. This never interfered with our ability to work together. In fact, the diversity in our ages was quite complementary.

    A: (For younger job hunters) Your question about my age seems to reflect some concern on your part. As you know, I have the experience and qualifications to perform well in this job. From my past experience, you can see that I am a very hard worker who learns quickly. I am willing to do whatever it takes to learn this job and do it well.

2. Q: Have you ever been arrested?

    A: That sounds as if you have some question about my honesty or integrity. I can assure you that I am an honest, loyal, and hardworking employee who will perform well in this job. Of course, I would be happy to provide personal references who can attest to my character.

3. Q: Are you planning to have children soon?

    A: I am a very ambitious, career-oriented person. I don't foresee that my personal life will, in any way, limit my desire or ability to work hard for your organization.

There may be times when you can diffuse the question with humor, but be very careful with this. You don't want to come off as flippant or sarcastic and make the employer think you aren't serious about the job.

4. Q: Do you have many debts?

    A: That depends on how our salary negotiations go!

5. Q: What does your spouse think of your career?

    A. He (or she) thinks I should come to work for you.

Other times, you may want to go ahead and indirectly answer the question, so that you can address the underlying concern more easily.

6. Q: Do you have any children?

    A: My mother takes care of my children during the day. I would be interested, however, in any day-care benefits your organization might provide.

If the interviewer does not accept your deflection and persists in asking an illegal question, you may wish to respond with a statement such as, "I don't understand why this is so important to you." If the interviewer can't give you a satisfactory explanation, you may have to politely remind him or her, "I'm sorry, but that sort of question is against the law, and I don't feel comfortable answering it." At this point, you probably already are having serious doubts as to whether you want to work for this company—if you aren't, you should.

71. Your Turn to Ask Questions

An interview is a conversation, not an interrogation. While your responses will be evaluated to determine whether you are the best candidate for the job, you must also actively determine whether this is the right position and company for you. In order to make that assessment, you, too, must ask the right questions to determine the answer. Here are some possibilities:

1. Can you explain the duties and responsibilities of this position?

2. What are the typical problems encountered in this position?

3. What qualifications would your ideal candidate have?

4. How long has this position been in the organization?

5. Why is it available now?

6. What kind of background and skills did the past person have for the job? Strengths? Weaknesses?

7. How does the company view itself within the industry?

8. What are the company's objectives for the future?

9. Where does this position fit into the scheme of things?

10. Who would be my supervisor?

11. Will I be able to meet or interview this supervisor?

12. What about the other members of the team? Is it possible to meet them, too?

13. How will I be evaluated?

14. What is the career path like for someone in this position?

> **HINT:** Always follow up your interviews with thank-you notes recapping your interest and qualifications for the position. Personalize this letter to each individual situation. If there is something you forgot to say in the interview, this is a good time to include that additional information.

72. The Top 20 Rules for Great Salary Negotiations

It is surprising how many job seekers think that employers are doing them a favor by offering them a job. The only reason for an employer to make a job offer to an individual is the company's expectation that the individual will help the company do what *it* wants done.

It is equally surprising how many job seekers gratefully accept an employer's first offer without attempting to improve that offer. This usually stems from the misguided belief that negotiation is not possible, that the salary and other terms of employment are a "take it or leave it" proposition, and that a job offer would be withdrawn if the applicant were to ask for more. Although there is no guarantee that you will get what you want just because you choose to negotiate, you can guarantee that you won't get more unless you try. The following guidelines should enable you to obtain a better package than the one that was originally offered.

1. Don't talk compensation before you have a firm offer. Until employers decide that you are the one *they* want, they have no interest in what *you* want.

2. Realize that salary is an expected negotiable item. Most employers expect to negotiate beyond the first offer. Try not to surprise them too pleasantly.

3. Negotiate in person with the hiring authority, whenever possible. Personnel representatives and search firm executives are not usually in a position to be as flexible.

4. Try to avoid mentioning your dollar needs first. In negotiating, usually "the one who mentions a specific dollar amount first . . . *loses!*"

5. Unless you ask, you won't get. Equally important, the more they pay for you, the more you are worth to them. Employers who "steal" you may look down on you later. Bargains seldom command much respect long after the purchase.

6. The position offer will *not* be withdrawn simply because you ask for more. At worst, the employer will remain firm.

7. Know your "bottom line" before entering into negotiations. Be confident enough to refuse the offer if your needs are not met.

8. Project that you are negotiating as a friend and an equal, seeking a resolution that is fair to both parties. It must be a "win-win" situation.

9. Negotiate base salary (plus commissions and/or bonus, if applicable) first. Benefits and perks come later. Typically, salary is the major cost factor and, therefore, the first point to be negotiated.

10. Provide yourself with a cushion in anticipation of being cut back through counterproposals. Normally, you should feel comfortable in asking for 15 to 20 percent more than the initial offer, or at least 10 percent over your bottom line.

11. If the offer is lower than expected, give positive feedback on your enthusiasm for the position, organization, and challenges, but *do* express your surprise and disappointment (not anger) at the offer.

12. Don't "negotiate with pistols." Never demand a concession or deliver an ultimatum.

13. Acknowledge your understanding that the other party must operate within certain constraints. Also, express sincere appreciation for each concession gained.

14. Don't trade today's guarantee for tomorrow's promises. You must meet today's needs from today's income.

15. Try to establish some backup options. Take an approach of, "If we can't do that, could we consider this?"

16. Negotiate benefits and perks in descending order of importance. Don't introduce a new issue until the previous one has been resolved.

17. If the other party is a skilled negotiator, relax! There's nothing a good negotiator enjoys more than negotiating.

18. Get the final offer in writing—even if you have to write it yourself and send it to the employer by registered/certified mail, with return receipt requested.

19. Don't accept the offer on the spot. Ask the employer for a few days to make your decision. This will give you some time to objectively evaluate the offer.

20. Only you can determine whether an offer is sufficiently attractive for you to accept.

Special thanks to outplacement consultant James Kacena for preparing this checklist.

73. Evaluating Job Offers

At last, you have a job offer. First rule of thumb: never say "yes" immediately. Express your thanks and interest; but take a day or two to make sure it really is the best offer for you. The following checklist will provide some guidelines.

		Yes	No
1.	Did I meet the person who will manage me?	☐	☐
2.	Can I get along with my new boss?	☐	☐
3.	Do I understand my job responsibilities?	☐	☐
4.	Are the responsibilities a good match with my skills?	☐	☐
5.	Will this position lead in the right direction for me?	☐	☐
6.	Is there room for advancement?	☐	☐
7.	Will I be able to strike a comfortable balance between specialist and generalist?	☐	☐
8.	Does the company seem to treat its employees in a manner I like?	☐	☐
9.	Is there a low turnover of personnel?	☐	☐
10.	Do I know why this position is open?	☐	☐
11.	Does the organization seem like a good match for my personality, interests, and values?	☐	☐
12.	Is the money acceptable?	☐	☐
13.	Is the offer consistent with industry standards?	☐	☐
14.	Are the employee benefits fair and competitive?	☐	☐
15.	Does the company seem secure?	☐	☐
16.	Is it in a growth industry?	☐	☐
17.	Does it enjoy a good reputation within that industry?	☐	☐

		Yes	No
18.	Will I be evaluated on a basis I find reasonable?	☐	☐
19.	Am I satisfied with the review process?	☐	☐
20.	Is the amount of travel involved acceptable to me? Am I willing to relocate, if expected?	☐	☐
21.	Will I receive training?	☐	☐
22.	Does the company pay for training?	☐	☐
23.	Will this job enhance my skills and career opportunities?	☐	☐

Once you have completed this checklist, review and summarize the positive factors—all the "yes" boxes.

_____

_____

_____

_____

Now, review and summarize the negatives—the "no" boxes. _____

_____

_____

_____

_____

Do the positives outweigh the negatives? (Be sure to think qualitatively as well as quantitatively. For example, opportunities to do challenging work for good pay may outweigh the disadvantages of a long commute. Or perhaps the money is a little low, but the opportunities for advancement and growth are great.) Try to evaluate whether the long-term benefits outweigh the short-term difficulties.

_____

When all this is done, ask yourself: "Do I want to take this job?" Only _you_ can determine the right answer to this question!

74. 9 Steps for Leaving Your Old Job Gracefully

At last, you have made your decision to leave. Regardless of whether you have another job offer or simply need a well-deserved sabbatical, it is important that you observe proper exit protocol so that you will keep your references intact.

☐ 1. Determine how much notice you would like to give. Two weeks is standard. For higher-level executive and professional positions, slightly longer may be indicated.

☐ 2. Tell your boss first before you leak the word to the office grapevine.

☐ 3. Schedule a face-to-face meeting with your boss. Prepare your resignation speech. Make sure that you keep it positive. Simply express your intention to leave, last day of employment, and appreciation for the opportunity to work with the company.

☐ 4. Try to negotiate the terms of your leavetaking fairly. Review your projects to determine an orderly transfer of responsibilities and which loose ends you can realistically tie up.

☐ 5. Offer to train your replacement. If you are not replaced by the time your last day rolls around, consider making yourself available by telephone for the first week or two after you have left.

☐ 6. After your resignation meeting, prepare your written resignation. Address it to your boss, with a carbon copy to the human resources department. Confirm your intention to leave and last day of employment. *Do not elaborate on your reasons.* Keep it short and positive. As part of your permanent employment record, it will follow you well beyond your last day of employment there. Make that memory positive.

☐ 7. Schedule an exit meeting with the human resources department to determine your benefits package. Review your insurance benefits. Determine your last day of health insurance coverage. If you need to take your health insurance with you, be sure to fill out the proper forms. If you are entitled to pension or profit-sharing dollars, make sure you know exactly how much money you are owed and when it will be paid to you. Again, fill out all necessary forms.

☐ 8. Beware of counteroffers. Review the reasons you decided to leave. If they are still valid, proceed with your plan of action and politely decline any counteroffers.

☐ 9. Handle yourself professionally and responsibly at all times. Termination often causes hard feelings. Never burn your bridges behind you. You may need references, networking contacts, or information later. If a cooperative relationship has been established, both parties benefit.

75. The Counteroffer Crisis

Your mind is made up. You have decided to leave your job. But your employer has other ideas and ups the ante with a counteroffer. What should you do?

1. Start by reviewing your reasons for leaving. Are you disenchanted with the pay, lack of challenges, insecurity, opportunities for growth? List your reasons here.

   _____

   _____

   _____

2. Review the terms of your counteroffer. Will it remedy your dissatisfactions or is it a short-term solution to a long-term problem? _____

   _____

   _____

   _____

3. What is the feeling behind the counteroffer? Does it feel like a genuine attempt to keep a valued employee or a short-term act of desperation? In other words, will you ultimately be viewed as a traitor who has no company loyalty? If so, your long-term potential with the company looks bleak. On the other hand, if the offer has been made in a genuine spirit of cooperation and professionalism, you may want to consider it. Record your gut reaction. _____

   _____

   _____

   _____

4. If you have a trusted friend or colleague within your organization, solicit objective feedback. How does it agree or differ with your opinion? ___

_____

_____

5. If you decide to accept the counteroffer, do you plan to stay with the company for a while? Or does this represent a stalling tactic on your part in which you will continue to look around for other opportunities? ___

_____

_____

6. Picture yourself working with your present employer for another year or two. How does this situation feel? Are you happy? Pleased? Angry? Discouraged? Sad? Bored? Record your feelings. _____

_____

_____

7. What is your past relationship to your employer? Have you always been treated fairly? Does the company keep its promises? In other words, will it "forgive and forget" if you decide to stay? _____

_____

_____

If you feel like you need more information to answer these questions, have a heart-to-heart discussion with your boss before making your final decision.

> **HINT:** Many employment experts believe that it is a mistake for job hunters to accept counteroffers from current employees. They believe that these offers are simply an employer's short-term solution to an immediate crisis and that people who accept that offer essentially kill their career with that company. They may never get promoted, these experts say, or they will be replaced at the employer's earliest convenience. This thinking is based on the outmoded notion that a job hunter is a traitor to the employer. Not everyone adheres to that mentality. However, it is important that you talk openly with your current employer before accepting any counteroffer. Make sure that there are no bad feelings on either side before you sign up for another round.

5

Changing Careers

"If we are ever in doubt what to do, it is a good rule to ask ourselves what we shall wish on the morrow that we had done."

—Lord Avebury, John Lubbock

76. When Is it Time to Switch Careers?

If any of the following circumstances apply to you, you may be a candidate for a career change.

☐ You were recently passed over for a promotion or fired from your job; you are thinking that this might be a good time to explore new horizons.

☐ You recently inherited a lot of money, won the lottery, became a candidate for early retirement, or made a fortune in a leveraged buyout.

☐ Your youngest child left home, graduated from college, or got married—leaving you with more time, money, or freedom.

☐ You have reached the top of your career ladder. You need new challenges and opportunities.

☐ You just celebrated a milestone birthday. Suddenly, you are thinking about your career goals differently.

☐ You recently celebrated some new success or accomplishment. This may give you cause to think about your career possibilities differently.

☐ You recently had a new baby. Now you are thinking you would like more time, freedom, flexibility, money, or job security.

☐ You recently have survived some personal or family tragedy. This gives you pause to reevaluate your needs, values, and priorities.

☐ Your interests have changed.

77. Where Are You Getting Stuck?

Now that you've determined you may be ready for a career change, what comes next? Do you know what you want to do? You're not alone if you don't. You may be getting hung up somewhere. Listed below are some of the most common complaints voiced by people considering a career change. Put a check mark next to whichever of the following situations apply to you.

☐ I don't know enough about what's out there to decide.

☐ Some fields look interesting, but I don't know if I would really like them.

☐ I have no idea what I'm looking for.

☐ I feel like I don't have any skills.

☐ My interests don't seem to translate into jobs.

☐ My values are in conflict.

☐ The jobs that interest me don't pay good enough money.

☐ I have no idea how to choose a career.

☐ I don't want to start over at the bottom.

HINT: People who want to change careers often run into resistance from family, friends, acquaintances, and employers. Sometimes this is the jealous green-eyed monster rearing its head from people who are too insecure to change careers themselves. Rather than try to convince them of the rightness of your desires, share your thoughts and plans with them discriminately. Look around for a support group of like-minded individuals who will encourage your efforts.

78. Figuring Out What You Want To Do

Planning a career change uses the same fundamental rules of career planning: self-assessment, job market exploration, and career decision making. Many of the checklists used in the career planning and job search chapters are equally applicable here. If you have not already completed those chapters, go back and fill in the following worksheets:

CHAPTER 1: Charting Your Career Path

3. 15 Work-Related Values

4. Interest Inventory

5. Personality Profile

6. Skills and Abilities Checklist

7. Working Conditions

13. Worksheet for Informational Interviews

17. Brainstorming for Job Ideas

18. 2 Forms of Career Research

20. Career Decision Making Worksheets

CHAPTER 3: Job Search Strategies and Techniques

39. through 65.   (Entire Chapter)

79. Returning to School

Many career changers return to school for new credentials in order to make their career transition. The following worksheet will help you determine how and if this option is feasible for you.

1. Once you have determined the career field you wish to enter, you must establish the exact nature of the training, education, or credentials you will need to make that transition. Have you contacted the professional association and talked to professionals in the field to determine its educational requirements?

_____

2. Have you investigated the programs that are available to you, including:

   a. traditional degree programs, taken on a part-time or full-time basis at community colleges, colleges, and universities

   _____

   _____

   b. individual courses at academic institutions, taken as a "special" student or on a for-credit basis

   _____

   _____

   c. professional development programs offered through professional associations

   _____

   _____

   d. university-sponsored workshops _____

   _____

e. correspondence or home-study programs

_____

_____

3. How can you support yourself financially? Have you looked into:

a. scholarships _____

b. grants _____

c. loans _____
(Note: Check with the school's financial aid office for information and assistance.)

4. Will you need to work to support yourself during school?

_____

5. Have you determined what kinds of jobs are available to you with your current set of skills? _____

_____

6. What about your family? Will they help with finances? What about emotional support? _____

_____

7. How motivated are you? _____

_____

8. What is your past experience with school? Is there anything in your past history that might prevent you from following through? _____

_____

80. Self-Employment Checklist

Self-employment offers the potential for independence, challenge, growth, and recognition. It also involves strong organizational and decision-making skills as well as the willingness to take financial and emotional risks, sacrifice job security, and accept responsibility. The checklist below should help you determine whether you have what it takes to succeed on your own.

- ☐ I am very ambitious.
- ☐ I have good emotional stamina. Rejection only makes me more determined to succeed.
- ☐ I have good physical stamina. I don't mind working long hours, even if that means nights and weekends.
- ☐ I have strong convictions and beliefs.
- ☐ I have good organizational skills.
- ☐ I trust my own judgment.
- ☐ I would describe myself as self-confident.
- ☐ I am a self-starter.
- ☐ I like working with people, but I don't mind working alone.
- ☐ I have good people skills.
- ☐ I know how to say "no" when I have to.
- ☐ I don't have trouble asking for money.
- ☐ I have enough skill and experience to run a business.
- ☐ Job security is not greatly important to me.
- ☐ I have or can obtain enough financial resources to build a business.
- ☐ I enjoy challenge.
- ☐ I thrive on responsibility.
- ☐ I am a risk-taker.
- ☐ I like to do things my own way.
- ☐ I am more of a leader than a follower.
- ☐ I have the time and energy to devote to a new business.
- ☐ My spouse and family would be supportive of my decision to start my own business.

81. How to Decide on a Business: 6 Steps

Susan Winer, a strategic planning consultant and past president of the National Association of Women Business Owners, believes that ideas for new businesses emerge from personal or professional experience. Career skills and expertise, hobbies, and extracurricular activities all can provide ideas for new businesses. So, when you are looking around you for new business ideas, start with your own experience. It's often the very best place to begin.

1. Review the self-assessment exercises from Chapter 1. Do your values and personality style point toward self-employment? _____

   _____

2. What skills do you have that would help you develop and operate your own enterprise? _____

   _____

3. Does your professional expertise lend itself to any specific business area or ideas? _____

   _____

   _____

4. What about hobbies or extracurricular activities? For example, lawyer Bill Daniels converted his photography hobby into his own location photography business after several years as a successful freelancer. Your hobbies and activities?

   _____

   _____

   _____

5. What about personal experiences? After lawyer Cheryl Heisler switched careers to become a marketing executive, many other attorneys began informally consulting with her about their options. She subsequently founded Lawternatives, a consulting firm that helps disgruntled attorneys identify alternatives to legal careers. Your personal experiences?

_____

_____

_____

_____

_____

6. Once you have an idea, you don't want to let your love for that idea cloud your vision to the point of unreality. You also need to check out its actual business potential.

    a. Refer to the telephone directory Yellow Pages to determine how many other similar businesses already exist.

    b. Network with your colleagues and friends for people you can talk to in similar or related areas. Set up informational interviews to learn more about their perceptions of the marketplace.

    c. Join at least one professional business owners association to take advantage of its resources. These groups often have networking opportunities as well as workshops and seminars where you can learn how to start and develop your business properly.

    d. Try to determine the range of your market by reading trade journals and contacting both government and trade associations for additional information.

    e. If you do not have prior professional experience in the field, you may want to consider working in it first. Part-time jobs, volunteer activities, internships, and apprenticeships all provide ample opportunities to learn the ropes before venturing forth on your own. That way, you can make your mistakes at someone else's expense.

82. Lateral Moves

Your ability to make a lateral move into a new position or industry rests heavily upon your ability to identify and sell your transferable skills. Transferable skills are usually general skills that you have acquired in one type of position, industry, or company, but that can be transferred into a different setting. Industry knowledge is often an overlooked skill which is particularly applicable if you would like to do a different type of work within the same industry or are interested in ancillary industries.

To help you determine which of your skills may be transferable, go back to Chapter 1 and review the skills and abilities checklist.

83. Informational Interviews: A Career-Change Cornerstone

Informational interviews sound just like their name. They are interviews you set up to gain information about specific fields, industries, and companies. They are a cornerstone of the career-change process because they help career changers reality-test their career choice by asking specific questions about what it is like to work in a field and how they can get into it. Since career changers often suffer from a lack of contacts, informational interviews also provide opportunities to meet people who work in your target field before you actually conduct your job search. Informational interviews are discussed in greater detail in Chapter 1, checklists 11, 12, and 13.

15 Questions to Ask During an Informational Interview

1. How did you (decide to) get into this field?

2. What do you like (or dislike) about the field?

3. What kind of training and/or education do you need?

4. What skills do you need (or use)?

5. Is the field growing?

6. What areas seem to be growing the most quickly?

7. What is it like to work here?

8. Can you explain the hiring process? Is this standard procedure for the industry?

9. What other kinds of places hire people from this field?

10. Would you mind reviewing my résumé and making some suggestions for improvements?

11. What is the best way to find a job?

12. Are there professional trade journals I should read?

13. Do you belong to any professional associations?

14. Can nonmembers attend meetings?

15. Would you recommend other people I might talk to about this career field?

84. 8 Job-Search Strategies for Career Changers

1. Use a functional or skills-based résumé describing how your skills fit with your job objective.

2. Conduct informational interviews to reality-test your career choice and establish a new network of contacts.

3. Networking should be your primary job-search strategy. Ask friends, family, and acquaintances to introduce you to people who work in your field of interest. Go back to your informational interview contacts for job-search assistance. Also, get involved in professional associations where you can meet people who work in the industry.

4. Direct mail campaigns may also be effective, but you must be very well-focused. Create cover letters that clearly explain your qualifications for the field you are seeking to enter. Of course, it doesn't hurt if you show that you have done your homework on the industry and company. The more individualized your approach, the more successful you will be.

5. Scan the publicized ads, but don't spend too much time on them. Responding to want ads puts you right in the heart of the numbers game. As a career changer, you will seldom look like the ideal candidate. In all likelihood, there simply will be too many candidates with credentials that are more closely related.

6. Don't waste much time on headhunters and employment agencies. They seldom will touch a career changer. Job hunting for career changers is strictly a do-it-yourself business.

7. Telemarketing strategies may also be somewhat effective. Again, it helps if you have a referral. Referrals generally guarantee that you will at least receive a fair hearing. In addition, phone calls give you a chance to create a discussion around your skills, whereas it may be harder to develop that sense of fit through letters.

8. Consider working with a career counselor. Most counselors are well-versed in the process of career change. They can help you identify when and where you may be getting stuck.

85. 33 Keys for Planning Your Career-Change Strategy

Once you have decided on a new field, you must plan your career-change strategy.

1. Can you enter the field without any additional education or training?

_____

2. If you need additional education or training, have you investigated the programs that are available?

_____

3. Will your current employer finance your education?

_____

4. If not, how do you plan to finance it?

_____

5. Have you applied for grants, loans, and scholarships?

_____

6. Would you consider changing jobs in order to work for a company with tuition reimbursement?

_____

7. If you can enter the field without any further training or education, have you identified the name(s) of jobs for which you can apply? (If your answer is "no," you may want to conduct further informational interviews to determine this information.)

_____

8. Have you identified your transferrable skills?

_____

9. List them. _____

_____

10. Have you written a functional résumé? (If not, what are you waiting for? Start working on it now.)

_____

11. Once you have written your functional résumé, have you reconnected with the network you established during your informational interviews?

_____

12. Have you identified the professional associations in the industry? (If not, refer to the *Encyclopedia of Associations*.)

_____

13. Have you contacted them for information?

_____

14. Have you obtained a membership directory?

_____

15. Have you started attending monthly meetings?

_____

16. Have you obtained information about annual conferences?

_____

17. Do they have a job bank?

_____

18. Have you submitted your résumé to their job bank? (If not, do it now.)

_____

19. Do you subscribe to industry trade journals?

_____

20. If so, do you read them actively in order to identify potential companies you might want to contact?

_____

21. Do you read and respond to classified ads in trade publications?

_____

22. Have you considered running your own ad?

_____

23. Which publication looks most interesting?

_____

24. If you cannot go directly into your new field without more experience (but you cannot afford school), have you considered apprenticeships, internships, temporary jobs, or extracurricular activities?

_____

25. Who might be able to help you with this?

_____

26. Have you talked to your alumni placement office?

_____

27. What about your networking contacts?

_____

28. Are you considering self-employment? (If "yes," please refer to check-lists 80 and 81 in this chapter.)

_____

29. How much time do you realistically think it will take to make this transition?

_____

30. Have you established goals in relationship to your career change?

_____

31. Write down your one-year plan.

_____

_____

_____

_____

32. Two-year plan.

_____

_____

_____

_____

33. Five-year plan.

_____

_____

_____

_____

6

Checking Your Progress

"Those who act receive the prizes."

—Aristotle

86. Charting Your Course

There is no time like the present to develop some concrete career goals. These may be in the form of salary increases, promotions, further education, planned job changes, skill development, or networking.

Sometimes goals evolve out of experiences that point you in new directions. It is important to be responsive to those changes. In the worksheets that follow, you will want to chart out your course as clearly as possible, then check your progress periodically to determine whether you are still on track. At times, revisions will be necessary and advisable. You may find in Year 2, for example, that you have developed some new skills that may cause you to revise your original plan. Or perhaps your career path has become clogged by the competition, causing you to reevaluate your needs. This may lead to a planned job change or a revised financial plan, depending on priorities.

Remember, goals are often interrelated. If you are planning a family, for example, this may limit your promotional goals in the immediate future. However, you still can plan for advancement later. Good long-term career planning keeps a number of factors in mind—but most of all, it develops a holistic view that integrates personal and professional needs.

87. Worksheet for Checking Your Progress

Start by writing down what you would like to achieve in the next five years—and how you plan to make those goals a reality. Try to be both realistic and idealistic. Let yourself dream. Set goals that are a little beyond your reach, so that you have to stretch a bit to get there, but not impossible to attain. Mark your calendar each January to review your progress and revise your plan, if necessary.

Financial goals

Plan: _____

_____

_____

Year 1 (indicate progress): _____

_____

Revised plan (make any changes for the coming year): _____

_____

_____

Year 2: _____

_____

Revised plan: _____

_____

_____

Year 3: _____

_____

Revised plan: _____

_____

_____

Year 4: _____

_____

Revised plan: _____

_____

_____

Year 5: _____

_____

Revised plan: _____

_____

_____

Promotion goals

Plan: _____

_____

_____

Year 1: _____

_____

Revised plan: _____

_____

_____

Year 2: _____

_____

Revised plan: _____

_____

_____

Year 3: _____

_____

Revised plan: _____

_____

_____

Year 4: _____

_____

Revised plan: _____

_____

_____

Year 5: _____

_____

Revised plan: _____

_____

_____

Education goals

Plan: _____

_____

_____

Year 1: _____

_____

Revised plan: _____

_____

_____

Year 2: _____

_____

Revised plan: _____

_____

_____

Year 3: _____

_____

Revised plan: _____

_____

_____

Year 4: _____

_____

Revised plan: _____

_____

_____

Year 5: _____

_____

Revised plan: _____

_____

_____

Job-search goals

Plan: _____

_____

_____

Year 1 (indicate progress): _____

_____

Revised plan (make any changes for the coming year): _____

_____

_____

Year 2: _____

_____

Revised plan: _____

_____

_____

Year 3: _____

_____

Revised plan: _____

_____

_____

Year 4: _____

_____

Revised plan: _____

_____

_____

Year 5: _____

_____

Revised plan: _____

_____

_____

Networking goals

Plan: _____

_____

_____

Year 1: _____

_____

Revised plan: _____

_____

_____

Year 2: _____

_____

Revised plan: _____

_____

_____

Year 3: _____

_____

Revised plan: _____

_____

_____

Year 4: _____

_____

Revised plan: _____

_____

_____

Year 5: _____

_____

Revised plan: _____

_____

_____

Skill goals

Plan: _____

_____

_____

Year 1: _____

_____

Revised plan: _____

_____

_____

Year 2: _____

_____

Revised plan: _____

_____

_____

Year 3: _____

_____

Revised plan: _____

_____

_____

Year 4: _____

_____

Revised plan: _____

_____

_____

Year 5: _____

_____

Revised plan: _____

_____

_____

Personal goals

Plan: _____

_____

_____

Year 1: _____

_____

Revised plan: _____

_____

_____

Year 2: _____

_____

Revised plan: _____

_____

_____

Year 3: _____

_____

Revised plan: _____

_____

_____

Year 4: _____

_____

Revised plan: _____

_____

_____

Year 5: _____

_____

Revised plan: _____

_____

_____

Other goals (specify): _____

Plan: _____

_____

_____

Year 1: _____

_____

Revised plan: _____

_____

_____

Year 2: _____

_____

Revised plan: _____

_____

_____

Year 3: _____

_____

Revised plan: _____

_____

_____

Year 4: _____

_____

Revised plan: _____

_____

_____

Year 5: _____

_____

Revised plan: _____

_____

_____

88. A Second Opinion

You probably have heard the expression, "There's more than one way to skin a cat." Similarly, there is more than one way to check up on your career progress. Try answering the following questions:

1. Am I meeting the objectives on my timetable? If not, why not? What can I do to make those goals a reality?

   _____

   _____

2. Are my goals realistic? Do I need to do some research to reality-test my assumptions? For example, perhaps salary surveys or informational interviews will help determine whether your rate of career progress is within reasonable limits.

   _____

   _____

   _____

3. Do I have the right skills and education to meet my career goals? If not, what should I do to change the situation?

   _____

   _____

4. Do I like my work? If not, why not? (To answer this question, refer to Checklist 39, "When Is It Time to Quit Your Job?")

   _____

   _____

5. Are my goals in conflict? If so, in what way?

   _____

   _____

6. Are my values in conflict?

_____

_____

7. What would be a fair compromise?

_____

> **HINT:** Keep a notebook at your desk, to be used exclusively for résumé updates. Every time you learn a new skill, participate in a new activity, or accomplish some specific goal, jot it down. When the time comes to update your résumé, you will have all the information in one place.

89. 7 Secrets
to Career Health

1. Update your résumé. Document any new skills, training, and/or achievements immediately. Otherwise, it may be difficult to reconstruct them later.

2. Network. Join professional group activities to meet new people and stay abreast of new developments in your field.

3. Grow. Take the initiative to learn new things. Volunteer for new assignments, sign up for training programs, or enroll in college courses. It will stretch your mind and improve your marketability.

4. Attend to your company's health. Heed early earning signs of "sickness" in the form of layoffs, cutbacks, or reorganizations. If necessary, look around for healthier places to work.

5. Evaluate your position objectively. Conflicts with bosses and coworkers, poor performance evaluations, or lack of promotions or salary increases are all warning signs that require your attention. Don't ignore them.

6. Promote yourself (tactfully). Talk openly about your accomplishments. This creates visibility and visibility breeds success.

7. Seek out a mentor who can teach you the ropes and protect you during times of trouble.

Conclusion ⸻

It is easy to become nostalgic for the good old days when a "one company-one career" mentality dominated the worklife landscape. Loyal, hard-working employees were virtually guaranteed a place on the payroll and a gold watch at the end of the rainbow.

Clearly, things have changed. Today's workers can expect to change jobs (and even careers) five or six times in the course of a lifetime—whether they want to or not. For those who prize securtiy, this is a very tumultuous time. Risk takers seem to thrive more in this climate.

In a workplace characterized by change and instability, there are no longer any guarantees. But there are rules to this new game that can and should be mastered. Perhaps the best job security of all rests with the individual's ability to develop good, solid career and job search skills, supplemented with the all-important right attitudes. Attitudes can make the difference between success and failure. Inevitably, those people who develop expectations of success fare significantly better than their pessimistic counterparts, because they see challenges where others see obstacles.

As a nation of workers, many Americans have been taught to be too passive and compliant about their futures. The great philosopher Aristotle was definitely on to something when he said, "Those who act receive the prizes." Hopefully, these checklists have supplied you with some of the ammunition you need to activate your resources and do the best you can. Good luck in all your career endeavors!

VGM CAREER BOOKS

OPPORTUNITIES IN

Available in both paperback and hardbound editions

Accounting Careers
Acting Careers
Advertising Careers
Aerospace Careers
Agriculture Careers
Airline Careers
Animal and Pet Care
Appraising Valuation Science
Architecture
Automotive Service
Banking
Beauty Culture
Biological Sciences
Biotechnology Careers
Book Publishing Careers
Broadcasting Careers
Building Construction Trades
Business Communication Careers
Business Management
Cable Television
Carpentry Careers
Chemical Engineering
Chemistry Careers
Child Care Careers
Chiropractic Health Care
Civil Engineering Careers
Commercial Art and Graphic Design
Computer Aided Design and Computer
    Aided Mfg.
Computer Maintenance Careers
Computer Science Careers
Counseling & Development
Crafts Careers
Culinary Careers
Dance
Data Processing Careers
Dental Care
Drafting Careers
Electrical Trades
Electronic and Electrical Engineering
Energy Careers
Engineering Careers
Engineering Technology Careers
Environmental Careers
Eye Care Careers
Fashion Careers
Fast Food Careers
Federal Government Careers
Film Careers
Financial Careers
Fire Protection Services
Fitness Careers
Food Services
Foreign Language Careers
Forestry Careers
Gerontology Careers
Government Service
Graphic Communications
Health and Medical Careers
High Tech Careers
Home Economics Careers
Hospital Administration
Hotel & Motel Management
Human Resources Management Careers

Industrial Design
Information Systems Careers
Insurance Careers
Interior Design
International Business
Journalism Careers
Landscape Architecture
Laser Technology
Law Careers
Law Enforcement and Criminal Justice
Library and Information Science
Machine Trades
Magazine Publishing Careers
Management
Marine & Maritime Careers
Marketing Careers
Materials Science
Mechanical Engineering
Medical Technology Careers
Microelectronics
Military Careers
Modeling Careers
Music Careers
Newspaper Publishing Careers
Nursing Careers
Nutrition Careers
Occupational Therapy Careers
Office Occupations
Opticianry
Optometry
Packaging Science
Paralegal Careers
Paramedical Careers
Part-time & Summer Jobs
Performing Arts Careers
Petroleum Careers
Pharmacy Careers
Photography
Physical Therapy Careers
Physician Careers
Plumbing & Pipe Fitting
Podiatric Medicine
Printing Careers
Property Management Careers
Psychiatry
Psychology
Public Health Careers
Public Relations Careers
Purchasing Careers
Real Estate
Recreation and Leisure
Refrigeration and Air Conditioning
    Trades
Religious Service
Restaurant Careers
Retailing
Robotics Careers
Sales Careers
Sales & Marketing
Secretarial Careers
Securities Industry
Social Science Careers
Social Work Careers
Speech-Language Pathology Careers
Sports & Athletics
Sports Medicine
State and Local Government

Teaching Careers
Technical Communications
Telecommunications
Television and Video Careers
Theatrical Design & Production
Transportation Careers
Travel Careers
Veterinary Medicine Careers
Vocational and Technical Careers
Welding Careers
Word Processing
Writing Careers
Your Own Service Business

CAREERS IN

Accounting
Advertising
Business
Communications
Computers
Education
Engineering
Health Care
Science

CAREER DIRECTORIES

Careers Encyclopedia
Occupational Outlook Handbook

CAREER PLANNING

Admissions Guide to Selective
    Business Schools
Career Planning and Development for
    College Students and Recent Graduates
Careers Checklists
Careers for Bookworms and
    Other Literary Types
Careers for Sports Nuts
Handbook of Business and
    Management Careers
Handbook of Scientific and
    Technical Careers
How to Change Your Career
How to Get and Get Ahead
    On Your First Job
How to Get People to Do Things Your
    Way
How to Have a Winning Job Interview
How to Land a Better Job
How to Make the Right Career Moves
How to Prepare for College
How to Run Your Own Home Business
How to Write a Winning Résumé
Joyce Lain Kennedy's Career Book
Life Plan
Planning Your Career of Tomorrow
Planning Your College Education
Planning Your Military Career
Planning Your Young Child's Education

SURVIVAL GUIDES

Dropping Out or Hanging In
High School Survival Guide
College Survival Guide

VGM Career Horizons
a division of *NTC Publishing Group*
4255 West Touhy Avenue
Lincolnwood, Illinois 60646-1975